Foreword

When I was a child, my grandfather was a mysterious figure. He appeared with the wind, sometimes from Germany, sometimes from Vermont, often fresh from a cruise. So strong was the aura of fantasy around him that at some point he lost a pinky finger, and I was sure it had been bitten off in a bear fight. I associated him with the extraordinary, because he seemed to conduct his life in such an extraordinary way.

As I grew up, and as my grandfather aged, my impression of him became less mysterious and more solid. The myths—about bear fights, and bicycle trips, about cruises and ballroom dancing—were replaced by reality. And it turned out the reality of my grandfather's life was more incredible than the myths. His childhood in Nazi Germany, his escape from the Russians at the end of World War II, his emigration to the United States and service in the Korean War, and his work alongside Werner von Braun during the early days of the U.S. space program, seem like the script of a Hollywood movie. That his daughter married the grandson of Jewish immigrants from Eastern Europe, and he counted his in-laws among his closest friends, proves that life is stranger than fiction.

Today my grandfather is 96, in possession of all his original joints and still enjoying a daily dip in the pool. His voice in this book—of someone who enjoys the food on an army base, describes his divorce with ease, and embraces as mere discomfort what most would count as torture - is entirely true. Whether these rose-tinted glasses are the greatest asset of his character, the secret of his longevity, a character flaw, or all three, is up to the reader.

Whatever the case, life really is his great adventure. We can all only hope to embrace life as fully.

Thank you, Grandpa, for allowing me the opportunity to get to know you better through this book. I love you.

Courtney Howard Hodapp
April 23, 2022

Foreword

Hans Merz is a member of The Village Writing Group at Presbyterian Village Austell—a group comprising residents who want to write about their most memorable experiences but need help in doing so. My role as facilitator and editor has been to provide that help. I encourage members to write their stories and read them aloud in our regular monthly meetings. Hans has shared many stories in essay form about his colorful life, first in Germany and later in the United States, but now he has written the sustained account to be found here. His title—Life: That Great Adventure!—lets readers know that his story, which he has written at age 92, will be unusual for the "end-of-life" genre. Hans writes with gratitude for Divine guidance, for his family and friends, and with conviction that he will be happy into eternity. As his editor and friend, I can say that Hans, with his optimistic attitude toward confronting life's challenges, makes the rest of us happy as well. We are grateful.

Mary O'Briant

Director, The Village Writing Group
 Presbyterian Village Austell
June 25, 2018

Life

That Great Adventure!

The Memoirs of a 20th Century, Transatlantic Man

Hans D. Merz

Soulstice PUBLISHING

books with *soul* • Flagstaff, AZ

ISBN: 979-8-9862457-0-6 (eBook)
ISBN: 979-8-9862457-1-3 (print book)

Dedication

This book is dedicated to my wonderful and loving family. First to my two amazing daughters and their patient husbands, Taryn and Alison and Bob and Tom. Next to my beautiful grandchildren, Courtney, Jordan, Taryn and Elyse. Finally, to the newest and cutest generation, my great-grandsons, Travis, Arthur, Lucius and Joseph. It certainly is a blessing to be surrounded at my age with so much love.

Contents

Acknowledgments

This book represents almost seven years of effort by a few important people. It would not exist at all without the Village Writing Group at Presbyterian Village in Austell, Georgia. They welcomed me in as a complete novice and encouraged me to start writing. Mary O'Briant kept me at it and typed each of the original articles from my hand-written drafts, correcting many mistakes along the way. It was her idea to consolidate them into a book of memoirs. Many thanks to Mary and my fellow writers for all their support. In fact, all the residents and staff at the Village have offered me the opportunity to be a functioning member of a vibrant community well into my nineties. I appreciate every one of you.

Once I decided to turn the series of articles into a book, Tom Singers, the son of Carol Singers, a Village resident, volunteered to type the revisions and help with editing. During this time, my macular degeneration worsened, and he was incredibly patient and supportive. Tom is now a dear friend, and I am so grateful for all his time and effort on my behalf.

Lastly, I thank my daughter, Taryn and her daughter, my granddaughter, Courtney, who I am indebted to for shepherding the book through the rest of the publishing process. They spent many hours on another round of editing and fact-checking, as well as helping me to remember the specifics about events and people. They also researched the publishing options and found the pictures. Thank you for all your work, patience, and support. It is because of all your efforts and support that I am still around to write this book.

Introduction

Without a doubt, life can be challenging and rewarding. Blessed with divine guidance, incredible luck, a loving family, and great friends I have made it to 95 years old. I have experienced a smorgasbord of never-ending games, and some times were tough. But thirty years into retirement I am determined to keep the action going, kicking "the box" down the road. Sooner or later the order will come down, "OK, your time is up, get in the box." Why hurry?

1949 West Germany. Aunt Babette, in the U.S. since 1927, agreed to sponsor me for immigration papers. The chance of a lifetime! It took some time. After all Germans were not on the top of the list during that period. In early 1951 I finally held a coveted visa and a ticket for a ship's passage in my hand. Before my departure a well-meaning friend sat me down. "Hans, you know, America is in a nasty little war in Korea, involving lots of warm bodies, many dying a hero's death. Wait until the storm blows over. You survived the horrors of World War II by the seat of your pants, don't push your luck." Good advice, but my mind was made up. Besides, as a newcomer they wouldn't want me. Ha!

Korea 1952. Hotter than hell. The central front, the Battle at the Iron Triangle. Each side pushing back and forth trying to gain an advantage over a few "strategically important hills." I was on water detail, hauling two five-gallon jerry cans up the hill to Able Company bunker on top of Sniper Ridge. I was dodging the occasional mortar round, which hit anytime, spreading deadly shrapnel all around. Sorry guys, no ice cubes.

How in the world did I get into this mess? After I arrived in the U.S. in June of 1951, I was advised to submit so-called first papers right away if I wanted to start the five year path to citizenship. That was all and good, except during wartime, citizen or not, Uncle Sam drafted you for two years. In September 1951 I was invited to visit the Draft Board office in Troy, NY. They had my citizenship papers and I had to register. To help soften the blow, they explained the benefits serving would offer after discharge: accelerated citizenship and the G.I. Bill. Also, excellent English classes. They even let me keep my German accent, which came in handy along the way. Since these all were consistent with my long-range plans, I signed up. With that I set the foundation for a sound future, albeit by way of another stupid war.

Obviously, I beat the odds again and returned to New York in one piece, ready to enjoy the fruits of my labor.

America, you got one happy new citizen!

1
Remembering My Parents
Starting a Career in Aviation
1926–1942

My father, Hans Merz, was an excellent musician, playing the flute and clarinet professionally. He learned the trade of a *graveur,* creating intricate etchings in copper for multiple applications at the Geislingen Metal Works. My mother Emilie was a wonderful housewife, seamstress, and creative cook during lean years. I was born on August 10, 1926, named Hans Dieter Merz. (As I grew up, I preferred my first name.)

We lived on the third floor of an apartment house in Pforzheim, Germany, adjacent to the Black Forest. These were modest facilities; times were tough in the 1920s, rampant hyperinflation. From early on, I was an active child, learning to use the apartment like an obstacle course. Well, one of my infamous actions almost turned into disaster. I moved a chair to an open window to get a closer look at the world, and after I had climbed onto the chair, I was just about to take the plunge to eternity when Mom, screaming, got ahold of a leg and pulled me back to safety. She also fainted.

She supported the family's budget as a seamstress and was busy. Most of her customers were families with children, so Mom was encouraged to bring me along. There were the Biebers, Burkharts, Webers, and more. Their kids, who were about my age, became my playmates—more or less my babysitters. According to Mom, I had a helluva time and never wanted to go home. My favorites were the Webers, who owned a watch company and lived in a villa with a pool in the ritzy section of town. I was drawn to the pool, not very deep, so we kids could really horse around. There were also delicious snacks.

When I was four years old, we moved to Stuttgart into a nicer apartment building on a busy street. Playing was not without danger. On one occasion—and I remember this vividly—I ran after a ball—right into the front of a slow-moving car. The driver didn't see me and knocked me right under the car; I came out at the rear, like I'd been on a conveyor belt. The only thing that saved me from being badly injured was that I instinctively kept my arms and legs close to my body. I was shaken up with a few bruises, and people helped me up to Mom, who, after hearing what happened, almost fainted again. Poor Mom! Well, I learned and became a little more street smart along the way. Most of my activities from then on were on the playground.

In 1932, we moved again, this time to a lovely area of the city up the hill (Stuttgart is surrounded by hills, woods and vineyards. Beautiful!) and a nice apartment on the bottom floor with a deck, easy to get in and out of. I loved it. As usual, I made friends quickly. They even had backyards to play in. Businesspeople were living here, with fancy cars. I was impressed. Many were Jewish—good Germans for generations—what was the problem?

Their trouble started right at the dawn of the Third Reich, in 1933. People enthusiastically welcomed Hitler, because he promised to get them out of misery with jobs, new currency, and so on—all badly needed. And yes, he delivered, to everyone's amazement, but he also voiced and emphasized a profound hatred of Jews. He thought they had caused all the problems. Wealth in Jewish hands was a thorn in his eyes, not to be tolerated. So, within months, many of my Jewish friends and their families just disappeared. We were told that they had left Germany because they didn't like Hitler. Period. There were other kids to play with, and at my age, life went on. But I missed them a lot.

1933 was the year I started elementary school (no kindergarten). School was about a mile down in the valley with numerous steps, easy to get down, hell on the way home. By the time I got home I was beat.

On the upper floor lived a gentleman, in his seventies, widowed, Herr Professor Ulmer, retired from the Technical University of Stuttgart. He made a big impression on me: tall, straight as a rod, and a walker with his cane. He encouraged me, with Mom's permission, to accompany him on his Sunday morning strolls up into woods, and boy, did he have interesting stuff to tell about nature and life. It even made sense to an eight-year-old. The most valuable lesson—and I never forgot—was: "Hans, always have empathy for others and live in moderation, never smoke, and you will enjoy a healthy, long life." Sadly, he passed away while we lived there, and did we miss him.

Hitler's first big program, along with improving the economy, was organizing the youth, the backbone of his newly envisioned Germany. Boys and girls, starting at age ten, were eligible to join his Hitler Youth. Of course, among the numerous activities offered, along with camping and sports, was indoctrination. Goebbels' propaganda was taught in such an ever-so-smooth and subtle way that you couldn't help but be enthusiastic. You were expected to be smart, loyal, strong, fast, tough—you name it—the up-and-coming super race, very competitive. My prize for winning a 3,000-meter cross-country run was an airplane ride circling the city. Just seeing Stuttgart from a bird's-eye view shaped my interest in aviation.

Vacations were usually spent with my grandparents, who resided in a small, very scenic city of Geislingen an der Steige, 45 miles south of Stuttgart. Their residences were only minutes apart. Since Mom's parents, the Mössmers, had more space, I stayed with them. My aunt Emilie Almendinger, whose son my age was a polio victim, partly paralyzed and wheelchair bound, lived with grandparents Merz. Cousin Erich, considering his challenges, was very positive and smart. We were great friends, and I spent many hours with him playing chess and cards he taught me. I also wheeled him around to see neighbors, an enjoyable time. My closeness to him was appreciated. I felt so proud of myself.

After spending time there, I had good excuses to run and see my other buddies, the horsing-around gang. We tried hard to stay out of trouble, but sometimes, you know, the best intentions ...... Our favorite playground was a delightful small stream, the Fils, with some swimming holes. We were forever trying to find something that would float, such as an old iron bathtub we confiscated at a farmer's yard. He used it as a rain collector. Early one evening, the four of us sneaked out with this monstrous tub and got it sort of floating. The trouble was it had a small leak. We came up with an idea. If you sat right on it, you could slow down the water flow. We knew it would never be navigable, but we made bets who could float longest and farthest before the tub was filled. Besides, this contraption was not stable and more than once keeled over. Anyway, somehow word got around about a missing bathtub. We were caught and received a hard dressing down, which we deserved. So back the tub went. The stream was still the main attraction. Floating down after a storm was a rotten length of a tree large enough so the four of us could balance ourselves riding it. It broke apart after a week's use. That was great vacation fun. Lucky that we didn't get hurt. I sure hated to go back to "civilization."

1938. Very eventful. My father enlisted in the Air Force (Luftwaffe), an important segment of Hitler's build-up of the armed forces. Dad had served in the German navy in World War I on cruiser Prince Eugen as the radio operator 1917–1918, and veterans were in high demand. After he completed training on the newly developed teletype system, we moved to Memmingen Air Base in western Bavaria, a fighter pilot school. A Sergeant, but with a very important job, Dad had to always be close to the Communications Center. As a result, we moved into one of the on-base apartments, reserved for officers. The apartment was sheer luxury, at least for us. Mom was ecstatic; I even more so. We lived next to a huge outdoor swimming pool and an athletic field. A perfect playground for a thirteen-year-old boy. Right off, I explored the base on my bike, sometimes straying into restricted areas and getting chased out.

To make some pocket money, I worked as a ball boy at the tennis court. I enjoyed being around adults but also had my friends my own age.

By September 1938 I was enrolled in the secondary education system, the Realschule, an eight-year, very demanding program (in my opinion). They really poured it on, science, English, Latin, Math, and more. Lots of homework—time-consuming and boring—I gave myself an order: Just do it! It worked, but my grades were never better than average. I had to live by schedules and time myself. (Although the whole secondary schooling took eight years, I completed it in six, the remaining two years waived due to my enlistment in the Luftwaffe in 1943.)

In May 1939 I had an appointment for a physical with Major Dr. Schneider, the base physician. His office was decorated with several handcrafted model sailplanes suspended from the ceiling. He noticed my gaze and mentioned that these were scale models of sailplanes they had on base, operated by the Luftwaffe Glider Club as a recreational endeavor. To boot, he was the club president. Of course I told him that that I wanted to become a pilot, remembering the impression that flight over Stuttgart made on me.

"Well, Hans," he said, "even though you are only thirteen years old, it's not too early to get a head start. Glider pilots are in big demand in the new Luftwaffe. They make better pilots with shorter training. So, let's see. I can get you started, with your father's approval, as sort of an informal member, hanging around, making yourself useful. We can always use a helping hand in the maintenance shop. What do you think?"

"What do I think?" I enthusiastically replied, "When can I start?"

"Well, come on out Saturday and check out our activities."

So, riding my bike Saturday morning to the flight line, in beautiful spring weather, I kept to the sideline and watched with amazement. They had six gliders/sailplanes lined up from the very basic to high-performance and a two-seater (side-by-side). The take-off method was something else again. A thin cable hooked to the nose of the glider was reeled in at high speed over a drum (winch) by a stationary engine located at the opposite side of the airfield, about 5,000 feet. The plane took off in a steep angle like a kite, rapidly gaining altitude to approximately 2,000 feet. What an operation!

After a while, Dr. Schneider noticed me, waved me over, and introduced me around. I felt so grown up. He informed them of the purpose of my presence. That was it! Welcome to the club. Did I find a second home? Yes. A thirteen-year-old boy could be impressed VERY quickly!

Later in the afternoon, Dr. Schneider pointed to the two-seater: "Hans, jump in. I'll give you your initiation ride." The side-by-side cockpit had two joy sticks, foot pedals, and a row of instruments. After he pointed out a few basic items, we took off, just hanging on the cable and seeing nothing but sky. What a feeling! At 1,500 feet, he leveled and disconnected the cable. We were floating practically noiselessly. He explained how a plane is controlled. The most important was the joystick, which moved in four directions. He had me hold it and just stir it slightly; it moved a little right, left, up, and down. Hey, I was piloting. Next the foot pedals. Pushing left for left turn, right for right turn.

The whole exercise lasted about 10 minutes. I closely watched how he landed, realizing that this is the most difficult part of flying. Well, it was over too fast. As I climbed out, I couldn't help but scream aloud: "WOW!" The guys standing around laughed. "He got you hooked."

What a glorious start of my aviation career. Numerous training flights followed, over time gaining experience, and Dr. Schneider let me fly this bird from start to finish. Along the way, I spent every spare minute in the maintenance shop, learning to work with tools.

Leisure time came almost to a halt when, on June 12, 1939, the family was blessed with a new member. Brother Eckhard had arrived. I had no idea about my mother's pregnancy. How would a 13-year-old know? They never told me. They just came home from the hospital, and Mom held a bundle in her arms. "Son," she said, "meet your baby brother."

What? A brother? I thought to myself: "Did we really need him?" (Not a nice thought), but here he was, changing everything. More home tasks. It was *sort of* a happy occasion. Grin and bear it. As he grew older and started to walk, he became my steady companion. I hauled him around the base on my bike to let everybody admire this ever-so-cute little boy. Sometimes I even dropped him off. Somebody always brought him home. I wished he had been 10 years older to be more "useful." Eckhard is now eighty-one, and we have a wonderful relationship. He lives near Stuttgart with his wife Herta and near their son, Oliver, and granddaughters.

Back to aviation: Germany had been fighting the war since September 1939. By late 1940 fighter pilot training had intensified, and the Luftwaffe started training kids my age. When I turned fourteen in August 1940, I was ready for bigger things than hanging around the Glider Club, and joined the local Hitler Youth Glider Group.

Dr. Schneider oversaw the training program I started in September 1940. We would be trained to the "C" level ending up as qualified glider pilots. To achieve this, the "A" and "B" level provided the basics. "A" training was accomplished on a hill via bungee cord take off and involved short hops, just to lift off ten feet and keeping the wings leveled and keep the bird in a straight line. Sounds easy, but you were the pilot and all by yourself. What a feeling! The glider for this very basic operation was called SG38 (School Glider 38). It was just wings, a plywood seat and open fuselage. You sure were exposed to the elements. After six "flights" each one longer and higher and more thrilling, you got your first wing, the "A". We were just young boys but felt like big deals.

For "B" level training, we moved back to the airbase because much higher altitudes were needed to accomplish the "S" turns. The winch take off method was used now. Nothing new to me because that's how I got started with Dr. Schneider in the GÖ4. The winch cable pulled the plane up to several hundred feet at an approximate 45° angle, and after disconnecting the cable you learned to make left and right turns in an "S" pattern, really moving the joystick and foot pedals. You were watched all along from the ground by the instructor and critiqued.

We could only train on weekends and in decent weather, so by the time all twenty of us completed the "B", it was October 1940. The "C" level training had to wait until Spring 1941. The winter months were spent with lots of theoretical studies, besides school-work, helping at home (remember baby brother). Our group, by then a tight-knit bunch of guys, were exposed to the Morse code communications system, navigation, more of the Führer's propaganda, and there was the glider repair and maintenance shop. They piled it on. Listen, if you are in a group with dedicated guys, it's just fun. My parents were very proud of me and gave me all the support and love.

As Spring 1941 arrived, our eagerly awaited flight training started up again. The "C" and final level to get the glider pilot license was on the schedule. The plane, a fully enclosed real-looking machine called Grunau Baby, take off method by winch system again to approximately 2000 feet, sufficient altitude to perform the "8" routine several times. All twenty of us didn't get through the training until fall of 1941. By gosh, we all made it without a mishap and received in a lovely ceremony our "C" (three wing) badge. The Luftwaffe had twenty aspiring future pilots.

Now the real fun started, because we were qualified to pilot any high-performance glider, called sailplanes, at any take off method on the hill via bungee cord, winch or, best of all, towed behind a motor plane to much higher altitudes where it was possible to locate (in the summer) the areas where you could utilize thermal updrafts (hot air funnels) above towns. Now you also had proper instrumentations to give you immediate information on what was going on around you. An easy way to find these funnels was to look for birds of prey and join them circling up thousands of feet and stay aloft for hours.

Along the way, I applied for enlistment in the Luftwaffe to become an officer and pilot. I was accepted and informed that my reporting date was April 1944.

My glider career ended with a big bang. I received permission to take my favored sailplane, the Mü13, to be towed to the Schwangau glider base, a 40-mile trip, located in the foothills of the Bavarian Alps. After release from the tow plane, I crisscrossed for 5 hours over mountain ridges staying aloft by sheer wind power, even circling King Ludwig's fairy tale castle Neuschwanstein.

2
WWII and Two POWs on the Run
1943–1945

I was so excited to report for active duty in April 1944. But first I had to serve, like everybody, three months in the national labor force, called Reichsarbeitsdienst (RAD). Very annoying, it was apparently all for the good of the Fatherland. I was scheduled for this "exercise" from November 1, 1943 to February 1944. The station: a small-town east of Munich. The RAD performed mostly manual labor on construction projects, of which we had tons. So here I was at the Eggenfelden labor camp with 160 other guys ready for whatever.

At this point of the war, Germany already had lost its edge. Allied air forces made daily bombing runs, and Munich was not spared, providing us with plenty of work, getting things moving, clean-up, even recovering dead bodies, all in the nasty winter of 1943–1944.

We even ran out of fuel for heating at the camp. Our leaders frantically tried to locate coal. Well, there was lots of it, but you had to get it. A detail was sent by train to a town in the Bavarian Forest to fill a wagon with one hundred tons of coal. I was one of the group, and it turned out to be the highlight of my RAD service. Wallern was a pretty little town and the location of an anti-aircraft training base, the trainees mostly girls. Wow, we couldn't believe our luck being quartered there. Of course, we were the big news and received a lot of attention.

Back to work. We came to get coal, and there were mountains in the railyard. We thought, why not two wagons? We called home and informed them. They in turn called the Wallern mayor who agreed with our idea. So instead of one wagon, we filled two which required a longer presence at our new-found home. We enjoyed this little vacation to no end and upon getting "home" were treated like big deals for our efforts. The remaining few weeks went fast, and I was discharged early March 1944. It was great to get home before starting my Luftwaffe career at Oschatz air base south of Berlin. I looked up my friends at the glider club who had some weekend activities and enjoyed several flights.

On April 1 I arrived in Oschatz (Saxony). Here officer candidates received eight weeks of basic training, like all recruits. There was lots of physical activity, hikes, workouts in the gym, firing range and—it never failed—political indoctrination in what an officer should know about the Führer's philosophy. The eight weeks didn't end soon enough.

The next station: officers' and flight school at the Luftkriegsschule (Air War School) Furstenfeldbruck near Munich. As it happened, the base was the pride of the Luftwaffe. Field Marshal Göring had apparently taken a deep personal interest in establishing an officers' training base modeled after the U.S. Air Force training center at Randolph Field, Texas. The base situated in the foothills of the Bavarian Alps, was impressive—nice quarters, sports and recreational facilities.

Training was tough right from the start, with Leadership School lasting two months—until October 1944. D-Day, of course, was June 6 of that year. The Allies had landed and fought their way through France. The German situation started to get very critical, massive shortages, especially aviation fuel. They found a way to make gasoline out of coal, which Germany had in abundance, but there were far too few refineries.

When our flight training started, it was a stop-and-go-operation. Plenty of time for officers' schooling, and training in navigation and Morse code. To accelerate pilot training, they came up with ground trainers—different cockpits with instruments and joysticks to duplicate real flight conditions, a makeshift operation which still required take-off-and-landing practice. Having had extensive glider training, I qualified fast to solo in different aircraft and received the basic pilot's license. But under what conditions?

The Allied air forces owned the sky. They didn't leave us much space to operate. Hundreds of "Flying Fortresses" appeared daily, making their bombing runs. By December 1944, our flight operations were limited to morning and late evening. It got scary on cross-country training flights; we were ordered to stay as low as possible. It got even worse after the U.S. introduced the long-distance fighter P38, "Lightning." They hunted us at any altitude. So, dear Führer, how much longer can we carry on?

What was the next level of our flight training? I always thought the Messerchmitt ME 109G was the ultimate of our fighter planes. Our aces loved it. Fast, reliable, a jewel! No such luck. Jets were the newest fashion. Six weeks before the house of cards collapsed, they called a group of us who were ready for fighter training together to be introduced to the Heinkel HE 162. It was something else again—a funny-looking small jet, the engine mounted on top, like a stove pipe behind the pilot. Designed and put into production in four months—and would you believe?—Hitler's big hope to win the war! Nuts! We were told that the BMW jet engine propelled this bird to 500 MPH, topping just about everything else in the air. It was even equipped with an ejection seat. So, when do we start? No way. The end was near. Forget the HE 162. Things changed rapidly, becoming desperate. By the end of March 1945, we received orders to pack our duffle bags to be shipped out on April 1, Easter Sunday. Destination? The Allied Forces were already closing in on the western front. It could only be the east, of course. They needed warm bodies for the final battle. Demoted from aspiring officers and pilots to the lowest military job: riflemen.

We boarded trains, and after many unscheduled stops arrived in Graz, Austria, to be part of a new division, formed from many different units. On April 17, the division had a strength of 11,000 men. One of the regiments—the 29th—included former cadets. Quickly trained to fire a bazooka and the semiautomatic M-15 rifle, we were supposed to be "battle ready" for anything. God help us. First by train, then on foot, hauling all equipment, we arrived in the Vienna woods, putting up defensive positions.

To understand this madness, the line consisted solely of infantry digging fox holes and waiting. The Soviets had just overrun Vienna with everything they had and were expected to arrive in our area within hours. Then, suddenly, new orders: the 29th Regiment was to be relocated. So, on we marched to the city of St. Poelten and boarded another train. Wow! What could they have in mind? We ended up in Brno, Czechia, loading on trucks, and a few hours later, reinforcing the 357th Infantry Division at the front line. At least that was the plan. But surprise, surprise, there was no front line anymore. The units of the 357th were in full retreat. We quickly got the hint and turned our vehicles around, heading west. It was complete chaos. No leadership. Of course, nobody wanted to become a POW of the Soviets. U.S. Army—50 miles away—please capture us! Could we make it?

It was stop and go. Sooner or later, we would be walking, because our vehicles would be out of gas. I figured if the Soviets were chasing us, we would be passed soon. And, by gosh, they did. Numerous tanks traveled at high speed through open fields, paying no attention to us. Several hours later, everything came to a halt. Word got through that our convoy had been encircled and was being captured. At dawn on May 8, under heavy guard, we arrived at the city of Deutsch Brod and divided into groups of several hundred. Luckily, I ended up with my old buddies.

Eventually a meeting was called, and a former German officer gave us some pretty bad news: "We are prisoners of the Soviets. Don't even think of going home. They have extended an invitation to be 'guest workers' somewhere in Russia. They call it 'rehabilitation work.' By the way, if there are any Austrians in the group, fall out. You are free to go home."

We wondered aloud, "Why?"

Apparently, there had been a special arrangement after the Austrian government in exile declared autonomy from Germany.

"Tomorrow, we will be trekking to Brno, about a three-day walk, to be loaded onto trains destined for Russia."

We looked at each other in despair.

Our Führer had left us facing hell, committing suicide with his new wife, Eva, on April 30. I never thought it would come to an end like this.

Next day, they issued German C-rations, consisting of a bag of hard crackers and a few strings of landjager (beef jerky). "Ration it," we were told. There must have been thousands of us in groups of 200 to 300 as we began our trek to east to Brno.

Now, of course, on everybody's mind was, "How can I get out of this mess?" Not a chance. Czech militia kept a close watch on us. They gladly assisted the Soviets, having gone through harsh German occupation for years. I could not blame them. At night, when we stopped for rest, they placed bright lights all around. How could they lose anybody?

After several days, my feet started to ache. Bad-fitting shoes gave me blisters. I had to slow down and was falling behind the group. It looked like others had the same problem pain, among them my buddy from flight school, Karl Heinz Meyerheinrich. We were a sorry-looking bunch.

Always on the lookout for an escape, I noticed the road getting curvier with woods on both sides. The group ahead had just disappeared around a bend. The following group was not in sight. A guard on a bicycle passed us and disappeared. "It's now or never!"

Screaming "Mensch Abhauen" (guys run!), and with everybody behind me, we disappeared into the woods. Forget the painful feet! Stopping after a few minutes and checking behind—nobody! We couldn't believe our luck and decided to break up in groups of two and scatter. I teamed up with Karl. Imagine, if we ever made it home, we had to thank our aching feet.

Our aim was to get as quickly as possible to Austria to make contact with German-speaking people, about a six-day trek averaging seven miles a day. Luckily along the road was good cover so we could stay out of sight. And there was traffic, mostly Soviet trucks. Despite our aching feet and lack of food, we kept going. Thank God we were free. It seemed like it would never happen. Eventually we saw a road sign: "Österreich" (Austria). With big anticipation, we knocked on the door of a farmhouse and identified ourselves. We were invited in, fed, and offered to clean up. Our feet also received some much-needed care. Things were looking better.

The family advised us to head toward Krems, on the Danube 40 miles away, and gave us blessings as they sent us on our way. Back on the road. Maybe sooner or later we would find a ride. Well, eventually, it came. A Soviet truck passed and stopped in front of us. Out came a guy who looked like an officer. Were they collecting stray POW's?

In broken German he inquired where we were heading. I did some quick thinking, remembering that Austrians had been released. "We are on the way home to St. Polten. We are Austrians," I said, smiling at him.

Would you believe it worked? He smiled back and invited us to hop on the back of the truck. He could take us to Krems. Here was the answer to our prayer. A 40-mile 5-to-6-day walk became a one hour drive.

After jumping off in Krems, we found a hotel, "Die Alte Post." Maybe we could check in. Let's try. A woman answered. We told her about our predicament, and she invited us in. Another lucky break. Although they were not open for business, we received the royal treatment. They let us stay for three days to recuperate. A mini vacation. (On a 1989 vacation to Germany I took a bicycle trip along the Danube, I looked up the Brunner family at the Alte Post, a unique vintage hotel, and stayed for a whole week. You can imagine that it was an unforgettable experience.)

In highly improved spirits, we continued our trek along the Danube, blessed with excellent weather. Although it was a busy road, mostly Soviet traffic, a parallel running footpath kept us well out of sight. To Linz, 80 miles. In no hurry at this point, just playing it safe—and there were plenty of villages on the way—we could ask for food and shelter. People helped us in every way they could. We enjoyed the awesome beauty of the Danube valley, like a couple of tourists.

Getting closer to the US-Soviet demarcation line, Karl and I received valuable information. According to terms of an understanding between the Allies, those who had been engaged at the Eastern Front would be POWs of the Soviets, and if they escaped, they would not be accepted by U.S. troops but immediately returned. This had happened to many unsuspecting soldiers at the Urfahr U.S. Army checkpoint, who assumed that the Americans would welcome them with open arms. Without this information, we would have fallen into the same trap. So, to avoid this problem, people familiar with the area provided us with a map showing remote paths. Although increasing our travel by miles, it kept us out of sight. In early evening, we arrived at a village on the U.S.-occupied side.

Next target: Paussau, Germany. We felt much safer, but in no way did we want to be picked up by U.S. Army patrols, of which there were plenty. Paussau was a five-day trip. Continuing to receive support from those we met, thank God, we were back in our homeland and not in Russia—just divine guidance, sheer luck, and determination.

Karl's home was in Hamburg, 350 miles to the north. I was headed west toward Munich. We decided to separate with a heavy heart. Through thick and thin we had become great friends. Afterwards, we lost touch – but I discovered in 2014 that he had lived a long and happy life, finally passing away in Melbourne, Australia in his 80s.

Now on my own, I continued, sometimes catching short rides. Walking on a major road, suddenly a U.S. Army jeep stopped. They wanted to see identification. Of course, I had no ID – the Soviets had taken it—and I was ordered to jump in the Jeep to be taken to the Erding U.S. Army camp.

After an hour's drive, they delivered me at the camp. Was I a POW again? Things didn't look too bad. I was assigned a cot in one of the barracks, where there even were showers, and was sent to a mess hall. Wow! Food!

The following morning, questioned again, with a German interpreter present: "So where did you come from?"

Again, quick thinking. "I was a Luftwaffe cadet in flight training at Munich Furstenfeldbruck Air Base. After the base was closed, they sent us to the Eastern Front in April. They kept us in reserve in the rear. When the war ended, the unit was dissolved. To avoid Soviet capture, we split. I ended up hiding."

Miraculously my flight school ID had survived, which I showed them. After the interpreter talked to his colleague, I was cleared, issued discharge papers and informed that I was free to go home. I couldn't believe it. That was the end of World War II for me.

I caught a ride all the way to Memmingen and found Mother and Eckhard, now six-years old, after a search. They had been evacuated from the bombed air base where we used to live and assigned quarters in a farming village adjacent to the city. We were so happy to see each other in good health and able to start a new life.

Sadly, my father was not so lucky. As a member of the Luftwaffe, he was one of approximately one million POWs captured in Munich by the U.S. Army at the end of the war and turned over to the French. He spent four years in forced labor camps. He never recovered – emotionally or physically – from the experience and passed away thirteen years later, in 1962 at age 61.

3
Times of Happy Baking and Dancing
1945–1951

Having survived the chaotic final days of World War II, and enjoying life with Mother and Eckhard, I wondered about the future. Nineteen, with an incomplete education and work experience – no one was hiring ex-Luftwaffe. Memmingen had no options. What about Stuttgart? A great city, although heavily damaged in the war. Why not check it out? Nothing ventured, nothing gained. We left in 1938 – me first, for Stuttgart, and a month later Mother and Eckhard, for her hometown of Geislingen.

We jumped on one of the few operating trains, all very crowded and very slow, for the 100-mile trip. I intended to look up the Mangolds, who owned a bakery. Their son Reinhold was my best friend when we lived across the street over an apothecary in the 1930's. Had they survived the war? I kept my fingers crossed.

In normal times, the streetcar would have taken me in a few minutes right to the Olga Ecke (Five Corners). To get to there now, basically walking over an obstacle course of damaged buildings and city ruins, was an hour-long trek. As you got further from the city center, there was less damage. Eventually I made it to the Mangolds. Once a four-story apartment building with shops, now everything was gone but the first floor, with a makeshift roof to make it livable. Lo and behold, the shop was open and looked very busy. Passing a line of customers, I went in and there they were, the Mangold family, greeting me like a long-lost son.

I spoke to Reinhold and his dad while they busily worked the line of customers. And busy they were. "Hans, need a job? We could use some help." Were they reading my mind? Without hesitation, I climbed aboard and never looked back. It would be a three-year apprenticeship, including health benefits and German Social Security.

As I mentioned, this was a very busy operation. Their shop, one of the few in the area having survived, was at the right place at the right time. The U.S. military city government operated several large and barely damaged buildings nearby for their employees, both Germans and Americans.

I had to learn fast. Pastry baking is a very diversified profession: cakes, pies, tarts, Danish, puff pastry and much more. But I enjoyed getting my hands gooey. With practice cake-decorating became my specialty and I was soon running the cake department. Since my mother knew the Mangolds too she was glad that I had found a "good home."

In Fall 1945 activity in Stuttgart picked up. There were mountains of rubble, so a massive cleanup was organized. Everybody participated. There were not many able-bodied men; the war had taken its toll. With great assistance from the surrounding farming communities, block by block the city was cleared—bricks cleaned for re-use, streets repaired, and the streetcar system put back in operation. That by itself was a huge improvement.

Surprisingly the 1945 local vintage turned out to be excellent. With plenty of local wineries, people started to get into the party mood. Were there better times ahead? You bet!

Dance studios opened again, offering basic dance classes and a great chance to meet girls, enhanced by the fact that there was a shortage of men. I enrolled, learning the waltz, foxtrot and swing. Overcoming an initial awkward time, but having great fun,

I was determined to become a dancer, and a good one. Girls like good dancers. Besides, it was great exercise. So after "graduation," I wanted more, lots more.

Along the way, I remembered that one of my flight school buddies was from Stuttgart. He was in the group of POWs who ended up in Russia. Assuming his family didn't know his whereabouts, I could at least let them know what had happened. Finding the d'Argents was not difficult, the name not being German. I looked them up and I had guessed correctly. They had never heard from Gerhard. I told them about the chaotic last days of the war: how we got captured, Gerhard most likely ending up in Russia, and how, by sheer luck, I was able to escape. Not the best news, but at least it was something. And did they ever appreciate it. They invited me back and we became good friends.

On one of my visits, I met the d'Argents's lovely niece Sonia who was my age. Chatting along, the subject of dancing came up. She had recently attended a basic course, too. I showed her what I learned; she did the same. Hey this is fun! Sonia became my dance partner. We decided to check out what was offered in advanced dancing. We found just the right place and enrolled. They even had a club-like setup with weekly socials and instruction. In addition to the English style dances (waltz, foxtrot, swing) and learning advanced patterns and style, they introduced us to the Latin beat, which had us hooked. The rhumba, samba, and cha-cha offered a wealth of dance possibilities so different, but so catchy. The music just wanted you to move the body in sexy gyrations, especially the girls. Yes, the Latins became our favorites. The fun never ended.

Eventually, the d'Argents were contacted by the International Red Cross and informed that their son Gerhard was at a labor camp in Baku, the Soviet oil exploration center on the Caspian Sea. They also started to receive occasional mail from him. Most German POWs returned from Russia by 1949. Among them was

Gerhard, and what a welcome it was at the Stuttgart train station. Can you imagine a group of ex-POWs being greeted by their families? Sons, fathers, husbands – four years after the end of the war. Sadly, many never made it home. War is hell. I could only thank the Lord, having been spared that misery.

My pastry job moved along nicely. After three years apprenticing, I passed the journeyman's exam. That completed my contract with the Mangolds. With their recommendation, I was hired by the Grande Cafe Planie for a one-year internship, fine-tuning and gaining more experience, including trade school. By chance I met the manager of the Hotel Graf Zeppelin who encouraged me to apply for the pastry chef job which would be available after their present chef retired. A great opportunity, but I wondered if I could handle it. Well, they gave me a chance and, after a break-in period with Mr. Lorch's support, I was able to run their bake department. It was a secure position with good pay.

I wondered if the pastry profession would be my life's work. By 1950, as things developed in Germany, it looked like a good choice. I kept an open mind for other opportunities, remembering my love for flying and the outdoors. A career change at age 24? Why not? It happened and fast.

Aunt Babette, my mother's sister who went to America in 1927, paid us a surprise visit in early 1950. She was widowed, no children, a businesswoman operating a large rooming house in Troy, New York, near Albany. Before she departed, she mentioned she would be happy to sponsor me to come to America, perhaps helping her running the business. What an offer!

My parents, who understandably were not wild about me leaving, came around when I explained that I thought America was my future. I had made up my mind. America it would be. Babette returned home assured that I would get there no matter what it takes.

As it turned out, getting my visa application approved was not as easy as I hoped. After all, I was sort of an ex-Nazi: a former member of Hitler Youth and the Luftwaffe. Certainly not a priority case for the U.S. State Department. But patience paid off. They came around. I had not been a senior official, had not committed crimes, and was not ideological. By May 1951, all the paperwork was approved. I was one eager kid prepared for anything. With "bon voyage" from my family and friends, a very happy life awaited me in the United States.

4
America and a New Life
1951

June 6, 1951. A tearful good-bye from the family at the train station for my trip to Rotterdam and on to the United States of America. My mother, of course, took it hard. Mom and I were always very close. All I could say was, "Mom, don't worry. I will be back." I had to think about my life and future.

When I saw the ship I was to board, I was in awe: the Dutch liner "New Amsterdam," one of the world's premier liners at that time. The seven-day Atlantic crossing was a treat—the food, facilities (even a swimming pool), and, of course, entertainment—dancing. This was the good life, traveling in style to my new country. The ship tied up in New York harbor. I was met by Aunt Babette, a lovely reunion. After completing the formalities, we had lunch at the German restaurant where my Uncle Fritz – Babette's first husband – had been the *maître d'*. The staff still remembered Babette and treated us to a welcome drink.

We made our way to Grand Central Terminal, past some of New York's famous landmarks, and then took a three-hour train ride along the Hudson River, to Troy in the Capitol District. The ride felt familiar, like journeying along the Rhine in Germany. Troy is a hilly old mill town but well maintained and the seat of three schools of higher education. Babette had told me about her "mansion," but when I saw it, the 100-year-old former mayor's residence looked very impressive, surrounded by a large yard. Babette had converted it into a 15-room furnished rooming house, and she settled me in a lovely room with vintage furniture. What a great first day in my new homeland!

Next day, first things first, according to Babette. I had to sign up with the Social Security Administration and submit my "first papers"—the application for citizenship. To become a citizen, you had to be in the U.S. for five years and, the earlier you applied, the better. It seemed like good advice at the time, but we were later to discover things were more complicated.

After settling in, I started to get busy, enrolling in English classes and doing some much needed repair work in the house. Babette was so glad to have an in-house repairman. Everything seemed to be working out.

Just outside of town, I found weekend big band dancing at the Crooked Lake Hotel. It turned out to be exactly what I was looking for, a nice crowd with mostly singles. Pretty quickly, I became known as that new kid on the block, with a German accent, showing off some cool continental moves. Back in Germany I had learned the importance of a firm lead, which makes it so much easier for your partner to follow you. I was glad to be back in my favorite hobby. It also opened doors for jobs. "Oh, you need a job?"

There was a new company called Conversions and Surveys, converting businesses and households from industrial gas to natural gas, which involved changing out every connection on stoves, heaters, and more. It was a nationwide effort requiring many technicians. I got myself into their training program and became a gas converter technician. Of course, to accomplish your job you had to have wheels. They helped me to learn to drive, get my license and a car. Now wasn't that the cat's meow! What a perfect setup getting around, meeting people, improving my English and a good paying job. My situation was almost too good to be true. Turned out it was.

In 1951, the United States was at war in Korea. Through the grapevine I learned that, in a time of war, if you applied for citizenship you were obligated to serve two years of military service. In mid-November 1951, not six months after my arrival in the country, I received an official-looking letter with the heading "Order to Report for Induction," signed by the President of the United States.

Greetings. Having submitted yourself to the local draft board composed of your neighbors for the purpose of determining your availability for service in the Armed Forces of the United States, you are hereby ordered to report to the Induction Station on December 4 at 7:45 AM.

Smack, there I had it. Take it or leave it. Having always been a happy go-lucky guy, I figured maybe it's to my advantage in the long run. Now I was going to be an American G.I. Who would have predicted this? Six years ago, I was wearing the Luftwaffe uniform.

At the Albany Induction Center, I received a physical which determined fitness to serve, and met other recruits, many of whom would turn out to be my future buddies. With a bag carrying three days clothing, I boarded a train for Fort Devens, near Boston, a sprawling processing center where I got my first taste of U.S. Army life: privacy gone; barracks; fall in, fall out; five minutes to do this or that; waiting in lines for everything. Did I really need this (again)?

But after a few days, it became routine, and I (sort of) enjoyed it. We had good food and camaraderie. While there I even enjoyed my first Thanksgiving. My favorite part was – and still is – the turkey drumstick. I'd been through all this before, so, in a way an old pro. The Luftwaffe had taught me all that stuff. Now I was a U.S.

Army recruit, Private Second Class, and my new profession: rifle-man. I knew I had to start someplace.

We soon left for sixteen weeks of basic training at Fort Riley, Kansas. I was impressed by the ride there, a train with Pullman sleepers and on-board service. At night the bunks were pulled down for great sleeping. After five days of sheer luxury, there we were in snow-covered and very cold Fort Riley. I asked myself why they got us here just one week before the holidays, since basic training wouldn't start until early January. Two weeks just hanging around? We were free to go home. Many did at their own expense. I decided to stay, and I was not sorry. There were lots of activities, such as dances at the Service Club, frequented by women from the surrounding area. I was even invited to people's homes. My first Christmas in the U.S. turned out to be a great time after all.

Serious business started January 3, 1952; in the coldest weather you could imagine. You kept moving just to stay warm. Firing range. Mock war games. Endlessly running the obstacle course. Long hikes with heavy gear. I learned everything an infantry rifleman should know in war action. Spring, and the end of this, couldn't come soon enough.

At the same time, I was enjoying myself. I received the Expert Award for shooting my M-1 rifle straight, and took an excellent English course offered on the base. The Army also enticed me into enrolling in a very special activity: jump school. Basically, parachuting out of airplanes.

Now who would want to do a stupid thing like that? Me. Always a sucker to do out-of-the-ordinary stuff, I applied, passed the tough physical, was sent on two weeks leave and ordered to report to the airborne school at Fort Benning Georgia on June 1, 1952. It I had only arrived in the United States one year ago. How time flies when you're having fun.

At Fort Benning we were informed that "jump school is a three-week course, physically very demanding, and many of you will not pass. If you feel that this is not for you, raise your hand and we will send you home." *Basta*. Since none of us wanted to be seen like a quitter, no raised hands.

The curriculum, and the Georgia heat, were intense. First was Ground Week, with the toughest never-ending physical activities like running, push-ups, and most important, Parachute Landing Fall (PLF). Otherwise known as contacting Mother Earth. It had to be perfect, or you could get really hurt. The second week was relatively easy – tower work using a 35-foot tower practicing plane exits, and then controlling the chute after being pulled up on a 250-foot tower. The third week included five actual jumps testing if you had paid attention during the previous two weeks. Along the way some of the guys, who initially didn't want to be seen as quitters, washed out. Only 60% of the class graduated – and after we received our coveted jump wings, we celebrated hard. I still cannot figure out how I made it.

Besides my wings, I received another present – my next assignment: Korea (why me?). I enjoyed another two-week leave at home and mentally prepared myself for more war action.

5
Korea
1952–1953

Back home at Aunt Babette's with my friends, I enjoyed my two weeks of leave. Getting into another war was not a pretty thought. Would I make it back alive or in a body bag this time? Just play it by ear, I told myself. According to my orders, on July 15, 1952, I had to report to Camp Stoneman in Pittsburg, California, near San Francisco. "You will receive an airline ticket with your orders. Pack your duffle bag, give everybody a big hug (don't get emotional), and enjoy the trip. Don't forget to make out your last will and testament." Is that all?

The flight from New York to San Francisco was something else. I was in awe to see the American countryside pass by in a Super Constellation, the flagship of the airlines. GIs on the way to Korea received first-class service. I ate it up.

The good-bye hugs from the stewardesses felt so good. The Army had me back. Welcome to Camp Stoneman—a sprawling processing center for Korea. At the gate, a big sign read: "We are in business to make your stay a pleasant experience." Wow! And they meant it. Everything was fast and efficient. The special services offered dances, shows, bus tours. On July 20th, several thousand of us Korea-destined "tourists" boarded the USS General Buckner, a World War II Liberty-class conveyance, battleship grey, with "luxury" accommodations. Twenty-four to a compartment, five bunks above each other. Estimated duration of the voyage: sixteen days to Yokohama, Japan, with a brief stop-over at Honolulu.

Life on board was so cool. Getting out of the bunk had to be done in sequence, the bottom guy first. The top one had to climb down on a narrow ladder. To keep your butt moving, you spent the day in lines, even for bathroom visits. Saltwater showers (so smooth for your skin). To get up to the deck for a sniff of fresh air, you were only allowed with your scheduled group.

After several days of calm seas, an announcement by the skipper: "This is the captain speaking. Folks, I must inform you, you'd better enjoy the pleasant weather, because we are fast approaching a severe storm, with rough seas. My advice: take the seasick pills and do not skip meals."

The storm came. It was a bummer. I didn't feel like eating, but I went to the chow hall anyway and—surprise—no lines. I ate solids as told. It helped for a while, but I couldn't avoid joining the sorry souls hanging through the railings. Having emptied my stomach, I went back to my bunk to sleep through the misery. Lo and behold, we survived.

After several days of calm seas, we sailed into Yokohama, the Port of Tokyo, and boarded buses for a ten day stay in former Japanese army barracks. We were ready to relax, enjoy real showers and "gourmet" food. Recreational services did not disappoint. There were interesting bus tours, even to Mount Fujiyama, and geisha shows for entertainment. Anything to make our lives more pleasant ahead of Korea.

We were informed that the main reason for this stay was to process us to our designated units in Korea. I met the guys assigned to the same unit—the 187th Regimental Combat Team. After another trip across the Japan Sea, to Pusan, Korea's largest port, we arrived at our destination.

At the start of the war in 1950, the United States and its allies were not prepared for the invasion. As a result, the Communists drove a weak Allied force nearly out of Korea. A small perimeter remained. It was fiercely defended until massive reinforcements of troops and equipment arrived and drove the Chinese and North Koreans up the Yalu River at the Chinese border. It was a fluid war period.

At the time of my arrival in 1952, all action was along the 38th Parallel. Trains transported us from Pusan to Seoul. The countryside looked war-ravaged. Seoul was completely wrecked. It had changed hands four times. Army trucks took us for the final trip to the war zone. The 187th regiment was located at the central front. After passing supply depots, tents for recovering troops in reserve, and just a few miles further up, the 187th headquarters, we eventually unloaded, stretched our legs and shortly after were welcomed by the regimental commander, Colonel Westmoreland, known to be an excellent combat leader. Good to know! (Westmoreland eventually became the supreme commander in the Vietnam War.)

The regiment occupied an area on the central front called the Iron Triangle which included two mountains, the Sniper Ridge and Old Baldy, strategically important positions. There were never-ending artillery and mortar barrages going back and forth, a noisy environment.

This was real war. I was invited to participate, joining Able Company on top of Sniper Ridge. Not a pleasant landscape. Without as much as a welcome, I was put to work repairing the damaged company bunker with sandbags, rocks, logs, whatever. This was my new home, sharing it with a bunch of my new buddies and some permanent occupants: rats. I was told, "They are our pets. Just feed them, and they leave you alone." Since the sniper ridge was a very steep hill, all essentials had to be hauled up manually. Man, they kept you busy. Hot meals were far in-between. You existed practically on C-rations, a box of "goodies," canned stuff, candy bars. We got a weekly trip to the rear area for showers and fresh clothing. My birthday on August 10 came and went, no cake, no party. What did I expect?

August 17, my first serious involvement. A six-man recon patrol with radio operator was sent out to pinpoint some of these pesky enemy positions we were exposed to. The squad was ambushed. To make escape possible, the radio operator Lester Hammond called for protective gunfire, which enabled the squad to escape through a ravine. Lester, who had been spotted by the enemy, was mortally wounded. Several of us went down with a corpsman and recovered Lester's body. We lost a great friend and a hero. He was awarded the Medal of Honor posthumously.

Things quieted down by the end of August. Early September our regiment received good news: We were to be redeployed to Japan, the southern Island of Kiushu, for extensive training in air assault operations. They airlifted us from Taegu Air Base to a base on Kiushu and from there by train to Kumamoto, a large city on Kiushu's west coast. We were to spend several months in Camp Wood. Just getting out of the war was a relief, and this assignment turned out to be a great experience. I received a new "job": radio operator of Able Company, which required extensive training on the portable radios, field switchboard, and telephones.

The radio was like a backpack, called "portable radio communication" (PRC-10). As the Company A communicator, I was basically the shadow of Captain Henderson, the company commander. On jumps, the radio was secured in a special pack suspended between the reserve chute and my feet. Training was intense: parachute jumps with heavy equipment, like jeeps and 155 mm howitzers, night jumps; we bivouacked, long hikes. Of course, there were fun times, too. Camp Wood was a well-maintained former Japanese officers' school with all the trimmings: Japanese-run mess facilities, post exchange, commissary, service club with dancing (band and ladies provided), chapel, and week-end bus tours. Even off-duty life was a busy time. I didn't want to miss anything.

My favorite trip was to Mt. Aso volcano where the U.S. Special Services operated a hotel nearby. This was also a good time to catch up with family correspondence, neglected in Korea.

The regiment returned to Korea in March 1953. Armistice talks had gotten nowhere. So, war with all its miseries continued. They put us back in the same area we were so familiar with—on top of hills, in bunkers, and you couldn't miss the sounds of war. We were just in time to join the "Battle of Pork Chop Hill." Our company bunker was on Sniper Ridge, practically next to Pork Chop, which the Chinese captured after we left for Japan. It was back and forth, and they threw us off Sniper Ridge. We had to retreat to the next ridge. Orders came down. We were to take it back because of its strategic location.

After air strikes and artillery fire, we eased our way back to the bottom of Sniper Ridge through ravines. There was little defense. They must have been running short of supplies and ammunition. As we approached, we were greeted with a hail of rocks. They were desperate. You heard it right. Rocks. Big ones, causing casualties. Eventually we recaptured the ridge. The company bunker was a mess and required repairs.

Action quieted down. But knowing the Chinese would be back, we couldn't let our guard down for a moment. Around July 20 we heard a rumor that they were just about to sign a cease-fire agreement - not a peace plan, but good enough for us battle-weary GIs. War action ceased on July 26, 1953. July. *Basta*, finished. All quiet on the Korean front.

We were relocated to a holding area – a nice camp with large tents, even cots and a mess hall with (at least for us) gourmet food like T-bone steaks. Man, that was the life. It was a very happy good-bye to Korea. They shipped us back home early October 1953. And it was on the good ol' General Buckner. Everything seemed more comfortable, even bigger bunk space. Man, this was cruisin'.

I was discharged at Camp Kilmer, New Jersey mid-November. Now I was eligible for immediate citizenship and college under the GI bill. I arrived back at Aunt Babette's just in time for Thanksgiving 1953, my first as a civilian, a proud American speaking fluent G.I. English with a German accent and looking forward to a rewarding life.

6
Home Sweet Home
1954–56

It sure felt good to be home for the holidays, having survived the miserable Korean War. I appreciated the comforts of life even more. I've said before, and I'll say again: *war is hell.* But I benefited greatly from my Army service. I intended to make good use of my quick citizenship and paid college.

Christmas was a wonderful time at Aunt Babette's. I will forever treasure her kindness to sponsor me to come to America and helped her in every way I could.

Most important, at the start of 1954, was getting my citizenship application to the Supreme Court in Albany. As a veteran, I received priority and ended up as a new sworn-in citizen in no time, with a ceremony. Next on my list was signing up with the Veterans' Affairs medical facilities. Getting around by bus turned out to be a pain, so I decided to buy some wheels, a 1953 Pontiac straight 8, automatic. It turned out to be a jewel, serving me faithfully for seven years.

First order was enrolling in college. Troy had two tech schools — the Rensselaer Polytechnic Institute (RPI) and Hudson Valley Technical Institute (HVTI). RPI was a four-year, highly rated, tough school. HVTI had a reputation as a so-so school, but it turned out to be exactly what the doctor ordered, offering a two-year college curriculum training people at the technician's level for hands-on jobs. Graduates were in high demand at GE, IBM, ITT, and others.

A subsidiary of New York State's university system, HVTI was in downtown Troy in an old brush factory. Sort of cozy, just a bunch of classrooms, labs, and a lunchroom. It was close to Babette's place, so I knew I would be able to walk. The student body numbered eighty, including many veterans. (Today, the college is known as Hudson Valley Community College and has a large new campus.)

There was one hitch: I didn't have a high school diploma. HVTI accepted the high school equivalent, which I would have to obtain through a tough, two-week course at Troy High School. Thankfully, I passed, and by September 1954 I had started classes as an electrical technology major.

Second order, with another six years of Army Reserve obligation, I joined the Troy Reserve unit, a signal company: weekly meetings, once-a-month week-end training, and two-week summer exercises at Camp Drum, in upstate New York. Hey, it was fun, and I made some extra money. My final rank was Sergeant First Class.

Third order, I needed a job. I saw an ad by Troy Arthur Murray Dancing School, offering specials. I checked it out, though I did not need dance lessons. How about instructors? The manager Dorothy Smith mentioned that they had an ongoing class for teachers, free for those who qualified. "So, Hans, are you an experienced dancer?"

"I took lessons in Germany."

"Well, let's see." She took me through the wringer in all standard dances: waltz, foxtrot, swing, Latin-beat rhumba, samba, cha-cha, tango. And did we tango! It was sheer ecstasy! Most steps in tango are international. We just clicked. I knew I was in.

The training class lasted several weeks. I had to learn the women's steps and was ready for action.

Now I had a job and social contacts. Teaching assignments were with single women; so many more women want to learn to dance than men, it's amazing. Men don't realize that dancing is an easy way to meet women!

One evening, Dorothy asked me to dance with a lady who was interested in teaching. It turned out she knew all the standards. We couldn't stop dancing. She sure turned me on. Love at first sight! Several weeks in training class and she was ready to teach. Her name was Jill Ambrose. We started to date. Dorothy would send us out to give dance lessons in country clubs and colleges. Jill also modeled for Lord & Taylor and knew her way around the clubs. Nice!

We started to spend a lot of time together and by fall 1955 decided to get married. Our engagement was on Christmas, planning the wedding for June 1956. These were really fun times.

Between all this social activity, I was attending HVTI. They crammed a lot of material into two years. The curriculum fit my interests perfectly – down to earth subjects like electronics, physics, math and English. Best of all, the job opportunities were super.

Ahead of graduation, the school arranged for job interviews. I had one with IBM that did not work out. I didn't care for their suit-and-tie atmosphere anyhow, so I went for another one that looked very interesting: the Chrysler Corporation, Missile Division. Their representative, a Mr. Zink, after introductions said, "You have a German accent." A good starting point.

Chrysler had recently been awarded the prime contract for the Redstone Missile System, developed by the Army Ballistic Missile Agency in Huntsville, Alabama, under the direction of Werner Von Braun (creator of the infamous V2 rocket in Germany). Von Braun had arrived in the United States in 1946 with many of his colleagues, by invitation of the Truman administration. Truman had second thoughts about Von Braun (who could blame him?) but went along on the advice of the Pentagon, which anticipated the future of rocketry as weapons. They also knew that the Soviets had a team of Germans with the same ideas. Well, Von Braun and his team got into the swing of things by using V2 technology and getting the Redstone (a 200-mile ballistic missile) off the ground by 1955.

Back to my interview: They needed technicians for their fabrication and assembly operations in Detroit, Michigan, at an old tank plant. I left an application which got the ball rolling. Mr. Zink promised to contact me. Several days went by. I couldn't believe it, but he called and informed me that the job was mine and to report on June 12th. Apparently, I was just the guy he needed. And they were in a hurry.

When he called, I mentioned the wedding on June 10. "Yes, it will be tight. Just delay your honeymoon." Jill, sitting next to me, overheard the whole thing. What I loved about her: she was such a good sport. "Hans, let's just get married, forget about the honeymoon, and get your job started. That has priority."

The wedding was a smash, simple, just family and friends at the Presbyterian church in Waterville, outside Albany. We left right after; they knew we were in a hurry. After a quick stop at Niagara Falls, we arrived in Detroit, reported in with Mr. Zink, and were treated to lunch and a tour of my future workplace. We were so impressed.

The job required citizenship and security clearance (classified work). Without my military service, this would never have been possible.

Everything turned out great. Settling in a rented house, our social life centered around the Arthur Murray Studio. We made friends fast. Jill became pregnant and, with great anticipation, she gave birth to our daughter Taryn, born on 23 March 1957. A very happy family. I started as an assembler and mechanic, going first through an intensive training program, theory and practical, then assigned to various fabrication departments for missile cable systems, on-board test probes, telemeters (sending missile performance data to ground).

I loved the versatility of my work. Chrysler was in the process to expand the Huntsville operations. I was transferred there in early 1959 and assigned to a department that did the prototype work on the newly developed Jupiter Missile, created by ABMA (Army Ballistic Missile Agency), a 1,500-mile missile system with nuclear warhead to counter the Soviet Union's aggressive actions in Eastern Europe and Cuba. In addition to the Redstone, Chrysler had been awarded the Jupiter contract—a huge project, and we worked overtime to get missiles ready for flight tests at Cape Canaveral, Florida.

I had planned for a rather lengthy stay in Huntsville, and we purchased a small, older home just to get settled. Things changed rapidly. Besides getting the Jupiter fabrication contract, Chrysler was awarded the installation project to commence in Italy and Turkey. Being members of NATO, both countries accepted the presence of nuclear missile systems within a 1,500-mile range of the western Soviet Union.

In the fall of 1959, Chrysler started looked for qualified people to perform the installations. Lo and behold, my boss offered me a job on the team—an estimated 2- to 3-year assignment, with family. After talking it over with Jill ("Did you say Italy?") I accepted. That was October 1959. Everything was well organized. Chrysler had us (wives as well) attend a course in Italian, rented our house and transported a team of fifty, including families, to southern Italy by mid-December. We were to be called United States Association for Technical Assistance (USAFTA). What an assignment!

Me as a young boy with my mother, Emilie Moessmer Merz and my father Hans E. Merz, at the Kur Park. My father, a musician, was playing with the orchestra in the park that evening. (*Image courtesy of author*)

In Geislingen, me as a young boy with my mother, Emilie Moessmer Merz, her sister Gretel Moessmer Kohn, their father Wilhelm Moessmer and his second wife Marie Magdalene Haug. (*Image courtesy of author*)

Photo of Stuttgarter Strasse in Geislingen an der Steige, the Moessmer Family Home can be seen on left. (*Image courtesy of author*)

Photo of me and Eckhard, circa 1940. (*Image courtesy of author*)

My father, Hans E. Merz, in military uniform, circa 1940s. (*Image courtesy of author*)

Me at Reich Labour Service, in Eggenfelden, Germany, 1944. (*Image courtesy of author*)

My favorite sailplane, Mü13, circa 1944. (*Image courtesy of the author, taken by Reinhold Mangold*)

Postcard of gliders over Neuschwanstein. (*Postcard, courtesy of author*)

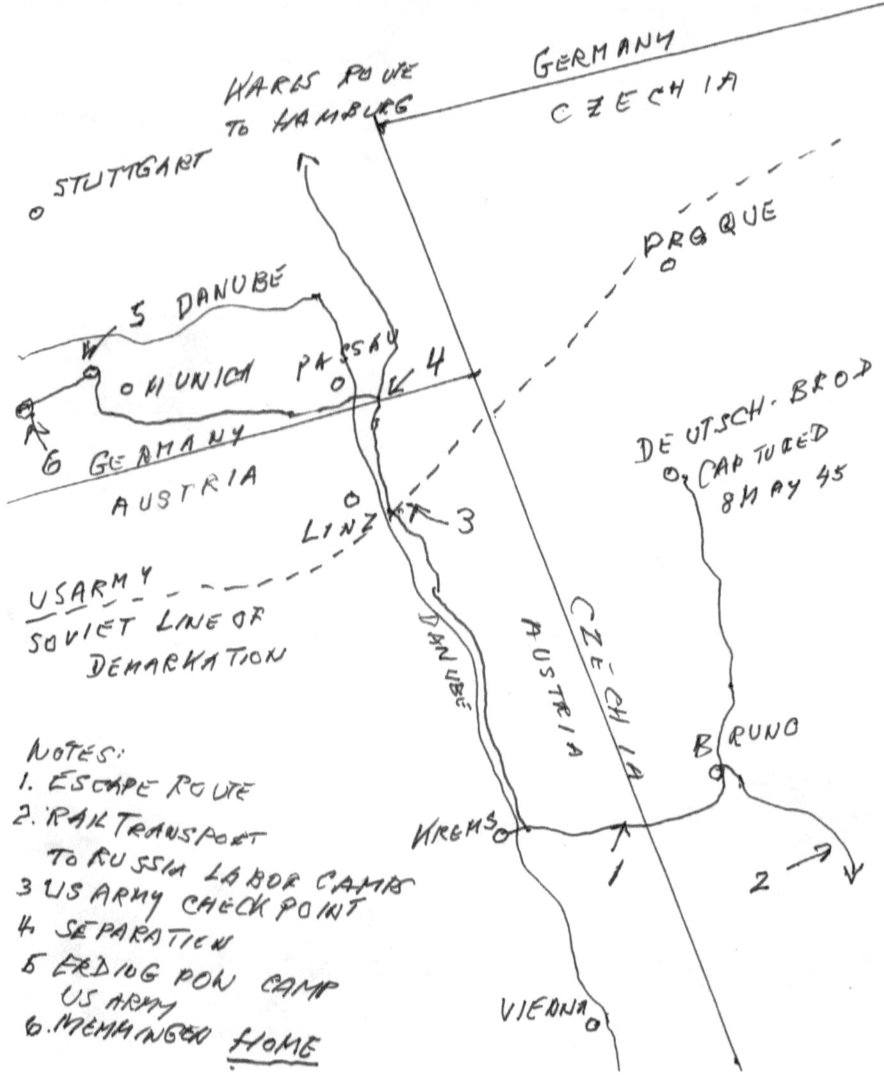

Handrawn map of our escape from Deutsch Brod. (*Image courtesy of author*)

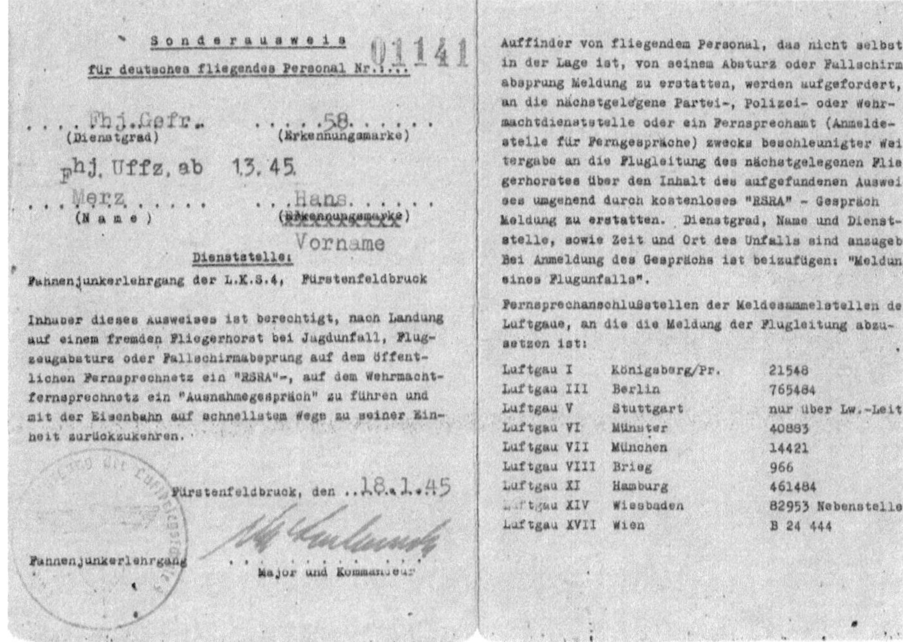

Furstenfeldbruck ID (from Flight Training) that gave me passage home after encountering the U.S. Army. (*Image courtesy of author*)

Me and my daughter Taryn in October 2015 across the street from the building that once housed the Mangold's bakery. (*Image courtesy of author*)

In front of the Grand Café Planie, the bakery where I apprenticed as pastry chef 1949-50, in 2015. (*Image courtesy of author*)

When I moved to America, I lived with my Aunt Babette in her home, 222 9th St, in Troy, NY (1954). (*Image courtesy of author*)

Manning the radio for Able Company, Korea, 1953. (*Image courtesy of author*)

A photo of my fellow troops in Able Company, taken immediately after my jump, circa 1953. (*Image courtesy of author*)

Making friends in Korea, circa 1953. (*Image courtesy of author*)

Wedding Day, Jermain Memorial Presbyterian Church, Watervliet, NY June 10, 1956. (*Image courtesy of author*)

Proudest father in the world, with Taryn, August 1957. (*Image courtesy of author*)

Our first home in Huntsville, AL, 2402 Pansy St, June 1959. (*Image courtesy of author*)

My parents hiking in the Alps, 1960. (*Image courtesy of author*)

Jill and Taryn in front of the Von Steuben Hotel in Weisbaden, May 1961. (*Image courtesy of author*)

Aunt Babette with Taryn and Alison, in Babette's backyard, July 1965. (*Image courtesy of author*)

With Taryn at the Leaning Tower of Pisa, May 1961. (*Image courtesy of author*)

My family celebrating my mother's 80th birthday, from left, back row, Herta, Manfred, Eckhard, Hildegard, Martina, middle row, my mother, seated, Herta and Eckhard's son Oliver, and Arman Schneider, September 1981. (*Image courtesy of author*)

Stuck in lava dust in Iceland, circa 1980s. (*Image courtesy of author*)

Descending Mt. Dundas in Thule, Greenland, circa 1985. (*Image courtesy of author*)

Thule, Greenland Wayfinder, circa 1980s. (*Image courtesy of author*)

Family vacation in Rottenberg - me with Alison, Tom, Bernie, Amy, Herta, Eckhard, Taryn, Bob and Courtney, 1988. (*Image courtesy of author*)

Skiing in Vermont, Smuggler's Notch, circa 1990s. (*Image courtesy of author*)

Kayaking in Vermont, circa 1990s. (*Image courtesy of author*)

Gentleman Host Dinner Attire. (*Image courtesy of author*)

Gentleman Hosting with June Allyson (L) aboard the American Queen, 1999. (*Image courtesy of author*)

Taryn's family celebrating my 95th birthday, August 2021. (*Image courtesy of author*)

Alison's family. *(Image courtesy of author)*

My first great-grandson, Travis. (*Image courtesy of author*)

A Christmas display in Paradise, Presbyterian Village Austell. (*Image courtesy of author*)

7
Jupiter Missiles in Italy and Turkey
1960-62

We were off to Italy feeling like celebrities. December 16, 1959 – a first class charter flight with stops in Newfoundland and Ireland. Destination Bari, a port city in southern Italy on the Adriatic Sea. And there was a welcoming party. They settled us temporarily in a fancy hotel until we could be moved into permanent housing. They were prepared. Plenty of information where to go, what to do. Members of the American/Italian Club were assisting us. We met the Salustros, local owners of a hardware store. We stayed friends throughout our stay in Italy.

Shortly after New Year's, the first meeting of the installation team was called. After all, we had a job to do and a huge one. The installation and checkout team had 18 months to get 10 bases operational. The sites were under construction and at different stages of completion. The first one and closest to the main base would be ready by March. In the meantime, we were to set up our shops in one of the hangars on Goia Del Colle air base—the staging area. Goia is located halfway between Bari and Taranto. Most families would be living in Taranto, Italy's naval port located inside Italy's heel. The first site was to serve as the test bed.

Next day, buses transported the working crew to Goia to have a look at the hangar we were supposed to move into. The subdivided areas would be ready in one week, so we could begin construct-ing shops for assembly and testing of the missile subcomponents, such as the telemeters guidance and control units and on-board sensors, which require elaborate test apparatus.

After several weeks of hotel life, we were contacted by the housing office that several apartment buildings in Taranto were ready for occupancy. We chose a fifth-floor furnished apartment with balconies and a great view of the harbor.

Our move was complete by the end of February. Glad to be out of the hotel. Jill and Taryn loved it. It was smack in the city center. People were very friendly and helpful. Jill could converse in no time. The guys never got too much into Italian; we had inter-preters. Taryn was now the bambino and getting spoiled with all the attention. We joined the natives enjoying restaurants, pizza joints, espresso bars. What a trip!

Looking for wheels, I got hold of a Ford, much used but driv-able. Since the car belonged to an American, transfer was easy. Buses picked us up for the one-hour drive to work. At the base, they set up a cafeteria. For lunch they took us to the air base's officers' club for three-course meals, including wine. They just put the bottle of red wine on the table. After several days, we had to cut down; our boss complained that our attention span was suf-fering. Too much of a good thing. Well, we just had to learn to adapt, sandwiches had to do.

With the shops set up and operating, we received the first mis-sile in June, and it was going into the test bed site. I was mostly involved with on-board equipment installation and checkout. Along the way, we trained the Italian Air Force personnel, who would take over the operations, excluding the warhead. Training took up most of our time.

Meanwhile, life in Taranto was great. Jill and Taryn explored the city. Jill enrolled in Italian classes. Even Taryn picked it up. Of course, it resulted in highly amusing dialogs with the locals.

By the time we left Italy, they could rattle off that stuff like natives. After several months, we traded the Ford for a new Audi 1000 SP (Sport). A 3-cylinder, 2-cycle engine was enough to give this baby speed and power to compete with any Italian hot rod (well, not quite). We loved that car. I eventually took it back to the States.

Our food intake was something else again. Pounds were sneaking up. What happened to that famous Mediterranean diet? We started to explore the countryside. On one occasion we adventured with friends to Naples, an unforgettable trip. And did we see the sites. Just driving over mountainous roads to get to Naples was a challenge. You know there are only so many hours in a weekend, but we managed to wander through the ruins of Pompei, the ancient city frozen in time. Next, Sorrento, over-looking the Bay of Naples. And to top it off, Capri, that world-renowned tourist haven. You just have to take a "cruise" into the Blue Grotto. The only thing free: unlimited sniffs of the lemon tree scent. Finally, the trip home over the death-defying Amalfi Drive. It took a week just to recover.

We were forever reminiscing about our Naples trip. Of course, there was a trip to Rome, the Vatican, Coliseum, and a horse-drawn buggy ride. During the summer of 1960, we ventured to Germany, the first time to see my parents since I left for the States in 1951. A long drive, all two-lane roads, well worth the effort. Mom and Dad and brother Eckhard were overjoyed to meet my family. It was a very happy occasion.

The first base was completed October 1960, three Jupiters in place, erected with all subunits installed and tested. The nine remaining bases were completed by July '61. After every site, the job got easier. While I was installing on-board equipment in an erected missile, the cherry-picker malfunctioned, resulting in an extended wait high above ground.

With the completion of the Italy Project, we were briefed on our next assignment—Turkey, five missile bases in the vicinity of

Cigli Air Base near Izmir, a large port city on the Aegean coast. We hated to leave Italy; it had become our second home. But a job is a job. Our belongings were packed and shipped. We stuffed the suitcases in the Audi, drove to Brindisi—a port at the Adria— and boarded a Turkish ship on June 10, 1961, heading for Izmir with a stopover in Athens, Greece. For Jill it was a miserable voyage as she was pregnant, due in August.

After having lived in a nice apartment, we were spoiled. They moved the families into a row of mobile homes (10 × 35) at Cigli. Jill was not too happy, and with a baby arriving shortly, we knew our time in Turkey would be much shorter. Was it ever hot—luckily, a very dry heat. At least the base (a NATO base) provided U.S. style shops, restaurants, movie theater and children's facilities.

To get to the city was an hour's drive. They had an Air Force hospital in Izmir, where on August 21, 1961, Jill gave birth to our second daughter Alison, a beautiful baby. The base dispensary had an excellent American physician who made house calls. We got great support.

Our mobile homes were parked along the base fence, providing a grand view of local life. There happened to be a much-travelled path for camel caravans, providing delightful entertainment for our children.

The Turks had a head start to get the five sites ready, making our job much easier. Most of our time was taken up training Turkish Air Force personnel.

We started to venture out in the Izmir area. The Aegean coastline was gorgeous: sandy beaches, camps, restaurants. Much of the area's history is Greek, formerly Smyrna, a distinctly European look. It was part of Greece until Ataturk liberated it. He is celebrated as a national hero and founder of modern Turkey. And there was Ephesus, dating back to 1,000 BC, one of the largest ancient cities, 30 miles south of Izmir. Visiting the old part of Izmir was one of our favorite shopping trips. The bazaar district had a wealth of interesting shops. Jill and Taryn had to look at everything. For real bargains you had to haggle. It was part of the game, and Jill was good at it. We always arrived home with "stuff," also delicious vegetables, hot peppers—one of my eyes burned forever after handling one and rubbing it. Though not as lovely as Italy, our time in Turkey would also become one of our fondest memories.

Ahead of the 1961 holiday season, we decided that Jill and the girls should return home. Mobile home life was just not the ideal place to spend the winter, so they returned to Albany, NY, to live with Jill's mother for the time being. Back in Turkey, we still had two more sites to complete. I sure missed the family, but my presence was required until all sites had been turned over to the Turkish Air Force, making sure that they could handle the job.

Leisure time now included exploring the area, especially Ephesus. One of our Turkish interpreters lived close to Ephesus and invited me several times to tour the ruins. I ended up with a few priceless pieces of ancient pottery.

My assignment ended February 1962. How did this huge project end? It was amazingly short-lived. Remember the Cuban Missile Crisis? The reason our Jupiters were in Italy and Turkey was purely as a deterrent to the Soviet Union's nuclear missile presence in Cuba, so close to the United States. The Jupiters were President Kennedy's bargaining chip, telling Khrushchev, "You take out your missiles in Cuba and we take out our missiles in Italy and Turkey." *Basta*. Mission accomplished.

Back in the States, I reunited with my family and returned to Huntsville for the next chapter.

8
The Apollo Moon Project
1962–65

Returning early 1962 from our 2-year assignment in Italy and Turkey to Huntsville, Alabama, was a pleasant surprise. The old cotton town was booming. The reason: NASA (National Aeronautical and Space Administration) had been established while we were away. Huntsville was on its way to becoming a city – new subdivisions, four-lane highways, shopping malls. It was the perfect time to go back. We moved back into our old, cozy house, which we had rented out while we were overseas.

It didn't take us long to realize we could afford something bigger and better, and the housing market was excellent. We looked at an area close to NASA's main entrance and found exactly what we needed. A three-bedroom ranch, full brick, central air, garage and most important, the price was right: $27,000. We bought it without hesitation and never looked back. Jill, an excellent housekeeper and interior decorator, had us settled in no time.

NASA's big project was now the Apollo Moon mission. The vehicle to get there: a huge rocket, the Saturn, to be created in Huntsville. I arrived at the perfect time. Chrysler Space Division became a prime contractor and had jobs – good ones. I went to their employment office, interviewed, and walked out with a job title: Data Acquisition Technician at the Saturn engine test facility.

I couldn't believe the salary and benefits. What a start – great homestead, great job. We were a happy family.

Now, how did this all get started? After the Soviet Union's early success sending several of their Sputnik satellites into space, the U.S. suddenly realized "Hey – we've got to do something." President Kennedy took charge of matters after the previous administrations had dragged their feet. He declared in 1961 that the U.S. would put a man on the moon before the end of the decade. *Basta*. It was easy for him to say, "Do it." But it took incredible efforts to make it happen. Of course, Kennedy must have had an inkling that there were people who had space travel on their mind all their life. It could be done. If there is a will, there is a way, especially with American know-how and money.

The place well-established in rocketry was the Marshall Space Flight Center in Huntsville, Alabama, home of highly successful missile projects, Redstone and Jupiter, the brain children of Werner von Braun and his colleagues. There was a team ready and able, utilizing to a great extent technology salvaging many parts of stored Jupiters and Redstones for a hodge-podge assembly, a prototype for the ultimate moon vehicle, the Saturn V.

Upon reporting at the newly erected engine test stand, a very secure area, I met my new supervisor and a company representative who would break me in. Good thing, there was a room full of consoles with monitoring and test equipment to record measurements and data of the engines being tested. "Good grief," I thought, "I have to maintain and run this stuff?" It looked complicated, but after some training, studying manuals, I got the idea. After all, I had lots of similar experiences with the Jupiter systems. After several weeks on the job, we prepared for the first hot test of five H-1 engines mounted on the Saturn S-1 booster stage. There were numerous probes to be installed in tight quarters of the engine compartment, such as gauges for vibration, pressure, temperature and stress. These were cabled to my equipment and in-turn remoted to the block house where they were monitored during tests. The block house was a bunker-like facility where all personnel assembled for safety during tests. The test came and went; everything worked as planned. Even Werner von Braun was in attendance. I met him; of course, we conversed in German.

To make a long story short, thirteen tests were conducted over several years, hot firing the F-1, a 1.5-million-pound thrust monster. Eventually, five F-1s lifted the 362-foot-tall Saturn V with the Apollo Capsule on top, carrying the astronauts to the moon.

Meanwhile back at the Merz homestead, we had settled beautifully. Our daughter Taryn started elementary school. We got around, partying, playing bridge. We contacted the Wry Dancing School, getting back into our favorite hobby. The summers were hot, so we spent a lot of time at nearby Guntersville Lake with beautiful picnic areas and beaches.

And we did some travelling. One unforgettable trip was to Texarkana, Texas where Jill's Aunt Lois lived on a dairy farm. We were treated to typical farm life with all the trimmings, including horseback riding. That was my first and the last time on a horse. Fun? No way, it was a disaster. They all helped me to mount the horse. Without a saddle I had nothing to hold on to but his mane, and I had a strange feeling he didn't like me. Now what? I made the cardinal mistake of squeezing my legs – whatever you do, don't squeeze your legs.

I know the darn horse was just waiting for a signal, because he blew his nostrils and took off like lightning. And where did he run? Straight to his stall through a narrow path, fenced on each side. I was scared to death. To avoid hitting the fence, I took a chance and dismounted at full speed, to hell with the consequences. Everyone came running to help me up, full of dirt and not without pain, laughing their heads off. Insult to injury. A photo of this would have been priceless. I just had to walk in the stall to give him a piece of my mind. He paid no attention, munching hay. Despite this, the visit was great. Of course, the girls loved it.

In the summer of 1964, we ventured up north to Albany, New York, to look up family and friends and enjoy the cooler climate. While there I happened to meet at the Plattsburg Airforce Base several representatives of ITT, who were in the process of installing advanced communications equipment called microwave, providing multichannel communications, and practically eliminating land-based communications. I learned that ITT's subsidiary Federal Electric Corporation was doing the same work in Europe for NATO, mostly in Germany, and they were hiring field engineers at their Paramus, NJ office. My ears perked up. Germany? It sounded interesting. I talked it over with Jill, who encouraged me to check into it. She loved Europe. One thing led to another. I contacted them and got hired. Just like that. Wow. My mother was going to be thrilled.

The decision to end my employment with Chrysler was not easy. This was a truly great working relationship. I took the responsibility of training my successor for several weeks, and they appreciated it. "If you ever want to come back, there is a job for you." Good to know.

9
Germany
1965–1969

was hired by the Federal Electric Corporation (FEC) for their European Tropo Army (ET/A) program as a Field Engineer. Arriving in Frankfurt in early summer 1965, I reported to FEC's German Project office. Jill, Taryn, and Alison were to join me later. Picking up roots and moving to another country is never easy. The house had to be sold, furniture put into storage. Jill had her hands full. But we were the adventurous type, just part of the game. Besides, we had plenty of previous experience.

My first assignment - not very technical. Since I spoke German and knew my way around, they made me a travel manager and tour guide for a team of surveyors visiting German military bases and surveying for radio relay sites—part of a large project to expand NATO's communications in Europe. Germany by then had recovered from World War II. The place was humming.

The tour guide job was fun, but I was hired to do engineering work and eventually ended up at an Army/Air Force radio relay site to be upgraded to a microwave radio station requiring a technical control facility. The site was located near the small town of Hohenstadt, south of Stuttgart, and, of all places, close to my mother's home in Geislingen. She invited us to move into her second-floor apartment.

After several months of separation, the family reunited in Frankfurt, a happy occasion. We sure missed each other. We enrolled Taryn and Alison in German school, and for transportation, I bought a co-worker's VW hatchback. And as a contractor representative working on military projects, I was entitled to utilize the nearby Goppingen army base for shopping just like back home.

The first project at Hohenstadt: install the tech control facility consisting of racks, consoles, wiring, cabling with test equipment for multiplexing/de-multiplexing radio signals, using manuals and wiring diagrams. Installation complete. Just a standard project. Next, get it operational, providing government facilities with telephone, teletype and data service via multiplexing and demultiplexing.

A short primer about what multiplexing accomplishes in radio communications. The incoming composite signal from the radio receiver is broken down by the de-multiplexer into many individual circuits and sent on to the user, such as a telephone, teletype and data. But before they can use it, circuits go through signal conditioning. The clean-up steps are tricky. It is the tech controller's job to check for and adjust proper amplification, frequency and noise levels. In multiplexing, the in-coming signals from the customer are combined (multiplexed) and sent in form of a composite signal over the microwave radios.

The family had settled in. After several months, I got a call to report to the main office in Frankfurt. "Hans, we certainly appreciate the job you are doing in Hohenstadt. That's why we called you. FEC just happened to be awarded a contract to upgrade tech control centers in Turkey. We need to send a team of experienced guys to get things started, and we want you to be a member of the team. Sorry, but this is an unaccompanied assignment."

Wow let's see. According to my contract, Germany was to be my station. Now with family, no way. "Gentlemen, I am sorry too, but I cannot accept your offer." Standing on shaky ground, I quit, signing some paperwork and giving them two weeks' notice. Out the door I went. Back in the car and calming down, it hit me. "Why did you just quit a great job?" Never mind, the girls were more important. Getting my brain into gear, I had a brilliant idea, which defined my life for the next 25 years.

The Air Force installation team I interacted with on the site was stationed in Wiesbaden, near Frankfurt. Their unit was GEEIA (Ground Electronics Engineering Installation Agency). This might be worth a visit. So, after an hour's drive to Wiesbaden Air Base and checking the bulletin board at the GEEIA's personnel office for job openings, one caught my eye: the position for an electronics technician GS-11. Let's inquire. "Yes, the job is available. You want to apply?" "Of course I want to apply!" I left an application. They gave me a bilingual thumbs up; my up-to-date security clearance and experience helped. "It will take a while. We will contact you." At least it was a start. I felt much better facing Jill with the bad news. But she appreciated my concern for the family. "We will manage." What a sport. I put in my two weeks at the FEC site, thank you. Now what? I needed a job until Wiesbaden came through, keeping my fingers crossed.

"Well, I'll try the German job market." So, off to the employment office. Yes, there was a temporary job available at a local chemical company for an electrical equipment installer. They were surprised to see an American. Well, after an interview (speaking the language did the trick, as usual) and with my German Social Security account still active, I was hired.

The laboratory was to be upgraded and expanded. My job was to wire up consoles for new equipment and activate. Hey, didn't I have experience with similar stuff? Without much ado, I fit right in, sort of a curiosity, born in the area, still speaking the Swabian dialect with an American accent. During lunch they all hung around to catch an earful. I loved the atmosphere. It was such a different experience.

At home, life proceeded nicely. The girls liked German school (it took a while), but kids learn fast, having so much contact. Taryn, being the older one, picked up, German in no time; Alison came up with a funny mix of German and English. It was delightful. My mother also was a big help. She had always loved children. In her twenties she was a nanny with a well-known Italian physician in Naples, teaching his children. Now she had a great time with her grandchildren and baby-sat when Jill and I wanted to get away.

My job at the lab progressed as planned. It took several months, but Wiesbaden came through. The job was mine – report for processing – just like that.

Of course, Mom was aware that our stay in Geislingen was temporary. I knew that she would hate to see us leave. "Sorry, Mom. We will be visiting as much as possible." And off we went to Wiesbaden, a three-hour drive, contemplating what our future would be. We had chosen a prime location. In central Germany, Wiesbaden was a renowned spa next to Frankfurt and the Rhine.

We were initially quartered at the Hotel General von Steuben, a U.S. military officer's hotel. My new employer was essentially the U.S. Government Civil Service. I learned that my GS-11 grade was equivalent to the rank of a major. I was in business. After several days, they settled us in a lovely furnished apartment and had our furniture shipped from Huntsville. Eventually we ended up in a two-story house in a small village close to Wiesbaden. Our daughters enrolled at the military dependents school, an extensive system for the large contingent of Americans in the Wiesbaden area. (It was the European headquarters of the Air Force.) I could not believe how everything worked out. A positive attitude is key.

My place of work: Wiesbaden Air Base, where GEEIA was stationed, with an engineering and installation division. The microwave radio section included the technical control department I reported to. The supervisor, Robert Tufts, welcomed me: "Hans, I am glad to see you. According to your resume, you are experienced in tech control installation and operation. We do planning and engineering. You are at the right place, and we are busy. Our customer is NATO, practically every country in Europe, and there are many bases requiring our service. GEEIA installation teams provide these sites with tech control facilities, mostly multiplex equipment. We provide the installation teams with so-called scheme packages which include floor plans for equipment installation, wiring diagrams, material list and installation instructions. For your first project, you will perform a site survey at Sahin Tepesi in Turkey: MC-50 Multiplex Overbuilt. We have a handbook on scheme engineering. Study it and prepare for the trip."

"OK, Boss." Would you believe, they had me on the way - destination Istanbul – ferry to Karamursel and up the mountain to Sahin Tepesi. I had contacted them ahead, and they were well prepared. GEEIA engineers, I learned, were a welcome sight because they surveyed for new stuff. This was the time for upgrading with MC-50 mux, presently the Cadillac of muxing: easier to work with, fewer breakdowns. They treated me like Santa. So the survey was a cinch. Making up sketches for new floor space, wiring interconnections, DC power, you name it. The final task: site concurrence letter outlining each party's obligations. Signed off by the commander. Man, it was fun - a worker's paradise. Short trips around Europe, producing scheme engineering packages. I could do it forever. Well, I actually did - for the next 25 years until I retired in 1991.

The family really enjoyed Wiesbaden. We had a lot of logistical support, shopping facilities run by the military, entertainment and travel. Living right smack in central Europe, of course, was the perfect place to get around, especially with the help of the military Rest and Recreation Department (R&R) offering many inexpensive travel opportunities. We visited Berlin, Paris, and went on skiing trips to Berchtesgaden in the Alps, where R&R operated ski schools.

And we absolutely had to experience the Oktoberfest in Munich, a blast. Jill and I even got away to attend a sailing course at Lake Ammersee in the Bavarian foothills. For camping, we adventured in our fully loaded VW hatchback through the Swiss Alps (no tunnels back then) and ended up at Lake Garda for a two-week stay. We found a beautiful camp on the south shore, with all amenities. As it happened, across from us camped a German family; their daughter Yvonne and Taryn became friends, leading to a permanent friendship.

In early 1970, the Air Force decided to wind down GEEIA's operation in Europe, relocating to the Keesler Air Force Base in Mississippi. It turned out to be a change we were not looking forward to, but a job is a job. I certainly wanted to hold on to this one. Life is not always perfect. Germany was fun while it lasted. Auf Wiedersehen!

10
Back to the States
1970–1990

The move back to the States went through, whether we liked it or not. The family ended up in Albany, New York, with Jill's parents and our furniture went into storage again. I arrived at Keesler Air Force Base in my car, with a few suitcases in January 1970. Everything was makeshift. Hurricane Camille had caused much destruction in August 1969, including extensive flooding for miles inland. Only a handful of my colleagues brought their families. Housing was very limited and often miles away, like in Mobile, Alabama. At the base, they managed to fix up a few buildings to provide office space. My quarters were a small motel room upstairs, the lower floor being rebuilt. Slowly—very slowly—life in the area got back to normal.

For recreation, I picked up a small sailboat—a Sunfish—just a board and the sail, but enough to spend some fun time sailing along the shore, avoiding obstacles, even stranded larger vessels. The beach was a mess, not a sight of nice, white sand. To summarize: life was as good as you could improvise.

Along the coast toward New Orleans, it didn't look too bad. They had missed most of the storm. I took a few trips exploring the city. What a cool place! When I could get up north to see the family was a good question. I had to play it by ear. Our daughters started school, and Jill made the best of living with her parents for the time being.

Our organization had responsibility for the Air Force's communication over a huge area—all of Europe and the southern part of the United States. The guys from former GEEIA were mostly assigned European projects. I had a hunch that something in that neighborhood would come up. Lo and behold: Turkey. Hot job in Ankara at NATO's southern headquarters: tech control upgrading. Along the way, I became the tech control upgrading expert. It was neat work, always at great locations.

I prepared myself for a long trip. In Europe it was easy— hop on the plane in Frankfurt and fly nonstop to Turkey in three hours. Now it was Gulfport, Atlanta, New York, Frankfurt, and Ankara—a 24-hour trip. I was picked up by a government car and dropped off at my assigned hotel. The tech control people were Turkish nationals, speaking excellent English. With their support I was able to collect the usual data required to come up with the installation package. My hotel was centrally located, so I could see some of the city on foot, including the mausoleum of Ataturk, the founder of modern Turkey. Unfortunately, the smog was terrible.

Two weeks later I was back on my desk in Mississippi, enjoying spring weather, clean air and big news: a complete reorganization of Air Force's communication units. Keesler's communication area would be divided into two groups, one to be relocated to Oklahoma City, the preferred location of most. The other, including myself, were to go to Griffiss Air Force base in upstate New York, near Rome. For me it was a lucky break, just a two-hour drive to Albany. At least I could spend weekends with my family.

Soon after Jill informed me that she did not want to move to Rome. In fact, she wanted a divorce. I had the feeling that something like this was developing. We had been growing apart for some time. We went through with the divorce and decided to stay friends. Jill remarried. I was invited to the wedding. My wedding gift was a three-layer cake, showing off my ex-pastry-chef skills. Unfortunately, her husband, Joe Zizzi, passed away after less than a year. It was not an easy time for the family. I made it a point to support them and stick around. In Rome, I bought a mobile home in a park adjacent to the base.

They located us in nice offices, big open spaces. This was a beautiful area at the edge of the scenic Adirondack mountains, which make the upstate New York so attractive—in the summer, with all the lakes offering great water sports; in the winter, cross-country skiing. The base even had an indoor swimming pool where I spent my lunchtime, truly an exerciser's paradise.

There were many weekend visits to the family. Jill had a beautiful home with a large back yard and in-ground pool. We had great times, and there was a new addition—a dog they rescued from drowning while boating in the Hudson River. It was just a mutt named Troy but the most lovable, playful pet, and a steady companion on my strolls. As soon as I walked in the house, he would run to get his leash. It was a riot! Jill and I got along much better now. Taryn and Alison participated in many activities. Somehow things worked out.

At work, I was transferred to the Cryptographic Systems Department. I always enjoyed new challenges, and this was sort of a promotion. First thing, they sent me to Crypto School—a two-month seminar at Lackland Air Force Base in San Antonio, Texas. The course covered cyber security, facility design, with homework, an essay, and tough final test.

The boss had me apply for top secret (TS) security clearance, which was denied because I was not a native-born citizen. That made entry into high-security facilities a little more complicated. I had projects at the National Military Command Center at the Pentagon and its alternate in a cave someplace. The Air Force and NATO built a command center in an underground bunker in Germany. I worked four months with an installation team to build the Crypto Center.

On one occasion in Iceland, August 1981, I was part of a four-man crew traveling by car from Reykjavik to Hofn Air Station over 250 miles of gravel roads. No air transport was available due to a recent eruption of volcano Hekla. Road travel was restricted. We got stuck in lava dust blown over the road in the volcano's vicinity. People at the Hofn Air Station sent out a truck after we didn't arrive as scheduled. No cell phones back then. Talk about excitement on the job! The return trip was much better. We spent time at Skogafoss waterfall and the glacier above. This was Iceland at its best. When in Reykjavik, do as the Reykjavikians do and take a dip in the legendary blue lagoon, a steaming huge hot tub.

Talk about travel, the coldest I ever got was at the DEW (distance early warning) line at Thule Air Base in northern Greenland. Just to get there, I had to catch an Air Force C-5 cargo plane out of Charleston Air Force Base. The flight seemed to take forever. During World War II, Thule was a stopover for combat aircraft flying to Europe. When we arrived, I stepped outside, and my contact man was standing there holding the thickest parka for me. "You know," he greeted me, "it's 30 degrees below. Welcome to Greenland."

There were some sights. Even animals such as well-fed Artic foxes hanging around for food from the mess hall. The guys treated them like pets. Of course, I had to climb nearby Mt. Dundas, pulling myself up on ropes. Once on top, it was flat as a table, with signs: "Careful Steep Drop." I was told that they even played some golf there. The base facilities were superb, such as the quarters called Hilton Hotel, and clubs. You had to be careful not to become an alcoholic. Besides the job, there was just nothing else to do. I experienced two trips to Thule.

Then, just the opposite: Sunnyvale, California, south of San Francisco. The Air Force's famed Blue Cube—and that is what it was, a blue-colored, windowless huge building, so secretive. Working on my project and being closely watched. I also took the opportunity to do some sightseeing. And it was worth it, visiting Yosemite National Park, Monterey, with the fifteen-mile drive along coastal Highway 1, Napa wine country, exploring San Francisco. One week full of lifetime experiences.

After spending over 20 years at Griffiss AF Base with the Air Force communications, I decided to retire. With 27 years of civil service at age 65 everything fell into place, a nice pension awaiting me. I was ready for a new lifestyle and adventures.

11

Retirement: Vermont and Cruisin'

1991–2005

My office threw a lovely party for several retirees. "You sure you don't want to stay on for a while?" my boss said.

"Listen, Jan, it's been awesome, but some change is in order. I'm going to quit while the quitting is good and intend to enjoy my pension as long as I can."

For my retirement location, I chose Vermont. Good friends Betty and Kelly Mann, who ran a bed & breakfast inn near Stowe, had a vacant apartment over the carriage house. They invited me to move in. I fixed the place up, and it turned out to be the perfect bachelor hideout. The property used to be a farm before the Manns bought it, moving up from Syracuse a year earlier. They were also in the process of converting the barn into an antique shop. I arrived at the perfect time to help them along with their big project. This was January 1991, cold and very snowy—a winter paradise.

One of Vermont's premier family vacation resorts, Smuggler's Notch, is located two miles up the valley, open all year, practically a village by itself: five ski lifts, superb trails, and what I really loved, an indoor swimming pool. All the businesses in the area were members of the Chamber of Commerce, and they offered each other discounts that also applied to ski passes. After skiing and swimming, the sauna and hot tub felt great. The groomed cross-country trails were something else, crisscrossing through the woods. I should have taken downhill lessons to get more out of it but waiting in long lift lines and freezing on the chair lift was just not for me.

I spent a lot of time at the resort. There were two large water parks besides the indoor pool, requiring many lifeguards. One day, the pool boss asked me if I wanted a job, part-time. Hey, why not? I took the Red Cross lifeguard course. The water parks had pools for all age groups, including big slides. You really had to be on the watch. Kids love to horse around. Their parents did not pay attention. That's why there are lifeguards. After several years of doing this, I ended up as a pool host—better pay, not so much sitting on those tall lifeguard chairs. Checking people at the gate and keeping order, just moving around, was more fun.

Back at the inn, there was always something going on. Kelly started a summer business: canoe touring on the Lamoille River, perfect for boating and so scenic. It got to be popular. He even had to hire somebody to assist. I liked kayaking better and invested in a single seater. Sometimes I travelled with the boat on top and bicycle on the rear. Outdoor sports paradise!

Along the way, Taryn and Alison got married, and I am the proud father-in-law of two great sons-in-law: Bob Howard, Taryn's husband (my Jewish connection), and Tom Fontecchio, Alison's husband (my Italian connection). Could it be any better? Yes, it got a lot better. I now have four grandchildren and four great-grandsons.

One evening, just relaxing after a busy day, my daughters called. "Hey, Dad, you still like country life? How about something a little more exciting? We just watched an interesting feature on ABC 20/20 that was produced on board the legendary QE2 luxury liner. Subject: 'Gentlemen Hosts'—neat-looking elderly gentlemen dancing with single ladies."

Cruise ships had gotten wise to the fact that single women passengers have a better time if they meet unattached men on board who dance with them, bring lively conversation to the dinner table, and, in general, make sure they don't feel alone at sea on a Noah's Ark full of paired couples. After all, the "Love Boat" wasn't about reading a book alone in your cabin every night.

"Dad, this is right up your alley. You should check into it. The contact is Loretta Blake, Working Vacation Agency."

Now let's see. There are ships involved. I remember with horror the Pacific crossings on liberty troop ships to Korea, bouncing around in rough sea. I could not envision myself dancing on a moving dance floor, holding onto my partner for dear life. Maybe it's worth a call. Nothing ventured, nothing gained.

They sent an application. I completed and returned it, wondering what I was getting into at age 67. But hey, kid, dancing is in your blood. It didn't take long. I had a call from Loretta, the CEO of the agency. She would be meeting with a group of applicants in two weeks in New York City. Could I be there? Well, at this point, I said yes. My daughters were thrilled. Ahead of the meeting, I had to stop at a dance studio that she used for dance reviews. Every applicant had to attend. I was tested by a lovely lady on all the standard dances: foxtrot, waltz, swing, and my favorites, the Latins cha-cha, rhumba, and samba. I hadn't danced for a while, but I knew my stuff.

I really enjoyed dancing with her. Apparently, she did, too, because I ended up with an "A" and a star. Wow! Feeling very upbeat, I arrived at LaGuardia airport for the group meeting. There were six. As a starter, Loretta met with the entire group, explaining the ins and outs of cruise ship hosting. She placed hosts on eleven ships operated by Cunard, Holland America, Regency, even Mississippi steamboats. Afterwards, she met each of us separately. She commented on my dance test results—the key to being a successful host. I knew I was in when she gave me a hug and remarked, "Hans, they're going to like you!"

Now my newest job: dance, dance, dance. Olé! I spent the night with Taryn, who lived in White Plains, New York. Of course, she had to call her sister to tell her the good news. Several days went by. Loretta called, "Are you ready?" (Man, they sure didn't waste any time!) I was ready, waves or no waves.

"Well," she said, "put on your sea legs for your first cruise. I want you to go on the Regent Sun we use for new hosts, sort of an introductory. You will have fun. It's a popular trip from New York to Montreal and back, along the New England coast and up the St. Lawrence River to Montreal, with port calls along the route—a two-week round trip. The Sun is an older ship, not the fanciest but an economical way to enjoy a cruise and popular with single women. That's why the cruise director likes hosts."

Two weeks later, I boarded the Sun in New York harbor. We were four hosts, nice guys, younger than I. Two to a passenger cabin. Cool. We had all the amenities of a passenger. The cruise line provided air travel, dinner with the passengers, and shore excursions, along with beverage and laundry allowances. We were not compensated or tipped. I didn't expect it anyhow.

First night out was the welcome party. Dress: suit and tie, tuxedo on formal nights. Hosts were introduced by the cruise director in the ballroom. Behind us a seven-piece band, in front a large dance floor, and—best of all—a lively crowd of passengers, many single women in partying mood. Just great dancing and fun. To my delight, the band played all my favorites. It sure was up my alley! Taryn and Alison, you hit it on the nail. Thanks.

I wouldn't have minded if all my cruises had been along the coast, in smooth waters, which was matched cruising up and down the Mississippi on the fabulous American Queen steamer. But there were some rough ones across the Atlantic Ocean. Returning from the Mediterranean and entering the Atlantic, the Maasdam bounced around like a small boat. That went on for several days. Not much fun. Good thing they cancelled all activities.

The worst one ever was on the way back to Key West, a hurricane-type storm. They had a lobster-fest planned for dinner. Forget it!

I stayed on for ten years, making it through 35 cruises: Northern Europe, Mediterranean, West Coast from Vancouver through the Panama Canal, Caribbean. Several trips were more special than others, such as the 1997 transatlantic cruise on the QE2. Loretta asked me to work with a German television company, Channel 2, that wanted to produce a documentary on hosting for German audiences. I was chosen as the lucky host. Talk about stage fright! Do not look into the camera. Sometimes I got my English and German mixed up – very entertaining. But we succeeded.

Loretta's agency encouraged viewers to contact them if they were interested in cruise hosting. And there were numerous calls. I even had the honor of meeting them as a group in Stuttgart for interviews and dance tests. We ended up with some superb new hosts.

At age 78, in 2004, I got to the point where this game became a little too much and informed Loretta that I had decided to "retire." For good measure, she wanted me to do one more trip: the maiden voyage of the Queen Mary—a twenty-eight-day cruise from Southampton to the Canary Islands, crossing over to Barbados and up north, stopping at numerous ports in the Caribbean, ending up in Fort Lauderdale. It was a gala event all the way and a fantastic finale to my hosting career.

Considering the ten years on the seven seas and the fourteen years I spent in Vermont—such different places and circumstances—and that includes trips to Germany to see friends and family, especially my mother after she broke her hip, falling at age 94 and ending up in a nursing home and permanently in a wheelchair. We spent hours together on lovely walks through the countryside. Am I ever glad to have done this for her. She passed away at 97. God bless, Mom.

12
Atlanta
2005 TO THE PRESENT

Daughters always know best. "Dad, you are getting too old living way up North and far away from your family." I agreed. Whenever I have followed their advice, it turned out to my benefit. For fourteen years, I had a great time in Vermont. And now the Manns were selling their property. Everything fell into place to move on.

So, in September 2005, I packed up my Saturn, said good-bye, and drove off into the wild blue yonder—Atlanta. The Howards—Bob, Taryn, Courtney, and Jordan—had lived there since 1998. The Fontecchios—Tom, Alison, Taryn, and Elyse—had lived outside Tampa since 1998. Everybody was in the same direction and within a reasonable distance. We relocated my Jill to be close to Alison in 2010.

Taryn found a one-bedroom apartment in Kennesaw, Georgia. I liked it and moved in with furniture from consignment stores. Within a short time, I was settled again, enjoying a change of scenery. There were swimming pools, great biking and walking trails. What else did I need? Good health to make all the fun possible. I drove to Florida to visit Alison twice a year, and there were several trips to Germany. I had my cake and ate it, too!

Vermont was nice and all, but Atlanta is a beautiful city, called the "City of Trees," perfectly fitting my lifestyle. In Vermont, miles of gorgeous scenery. At Kennesaw, lots of trees outside my window, with a gorge and small stream.

Although I really enjoyed my drives to Florida, Taryn and Alison suggested it would be safer to fly. They were right, again. At my age, you never know. Now it's a twice-a-year Southwest flight, which limits my getting around at Alison's, but we manage. Just being with them is a treat.

Driving in Atlanta certainly is challenging, but I got through without a mishap. So not to push my luck, I decided to quit at age 93. It has been seventy years of driving pleasure. Now I just enjoy being chauffeured around.

As we all know, aging brings problems we have no control over. A high-mileage old engine needs upkeep. I learned that my aortic heart valve was kaput and needed to be replaced, and quick, via open heart surgery. I received a bovine valve. It's been over 10 years now and it's working fine. My low pulse (around 55–60) keeps it from doing too much work. Annoying dizzy spells caused me to end up in the ER a few times. Just drinking lots of water took care of that.

After living nine years in Kennesaw, Taryn thought it would be a good idea to check into retirement homes. She found something appealing on the internet. I even zeroed in on Google Maps. Worthwhile to investigate - just up the road on the East-West Connector, called Presbyterian Village Austell. So we made an appointment, and entering the property, a park-like environment, even with a lake, I was sold. The leasing manager, Michelle Morris, didn't have to do much selling. There was a studio apartment ready to move into. So, with that and an indoor pool to die for, healthy gourmet food in a four-star setting, including lovely fellow residents—did I want more? I was ready to sign in for the remainder of my life.

This was back in November 2014. Now, whenever I must venture into the outside world, I cannot wait to get back through the Village entrance, sometimes encountering our resident Canada geese in the middle of the road, making messes. They must be on long-lease.

Enjoying life for several months at the Village and looking at the activities program, I wondered how a dance class would go over. After proposing it to the Activities Committee, with their blessing, I planned a one-hour weekly session. Now, let's face it: I would be dealing with old folks, many limited getting around, some even in wheelchairs or pushing walkers. I kept my fingers crossed, and it worked out surprisingly well for over a year. I was the one who quit because of increasing hearing problems, causing my balance to suffer, and making music sound more and more off-tune. I started with a motley group—no "Dancing with the Stars" material, but very upbeat. I kept it simple. Playing catchy music, they could hum along, tapping their feet, just moving, and they loved my big band music—the old favorites like "One O'Clock Jump," "In the Mood," and "Stomping at the Savoy." When they tired, we sat down and got into lively talks, just reminiscing.

Several in the group were more into ballroom dancing, which required me to fall back to different dances, such as the Latin beat and routines I had taught in the studio. Lo and behold, two of my most enthusiastic students enjoyed dancing together so much they fell in love and tied the knot, treating us to a wonderful wedding reception at the Village Center January 1, 2017. Thank you, Lee and Faye McClary. We all enjoyed your wedding waltz, to the tune of "Fascination"—a happy conclusion to my "just moving to music" idea.

Talking about residents—I love them all, if only I could understand them. You see, several years ago I noticed that people talking to me were slurring their speech, talking too fast, not pronouncing the words clearly. Hey, what happened? Finally,

I realized, "Stupid, it's your hearing and a Catch-22 problem." I actually hear too much sound. Hearing aids make it even worse. So here I sit, getting an earful of noise but no speech recognition. And the worst is that sounds are distorted. I cannot stand music anymore. OK, if I must put up with this, so can everybody else. Sorry.

This did not stop me from joining a most delightful group of residents—the Village Writing Group—under the able guidance of Mary O'Briant, who tried to decipher my scribbles and comes up with perfect manuscripts helping me get this memoir together. Thank you, Mary!

I am ending this story with happy thoughts and a "thank-you" note. After all, I have lived a great, adventurous, interesting life with my wonderful family and friends. That's why I am donating my body to Emory University Medical School. Let the future physicians have fun poking around a vintage corpse. You guys better be careful – I am watching you.

Bon Voyage!